Fairbanks

CITY HISTORY SERIES

Anchorage
Fairbanks

CITY HISTORY SERIES

A GOLD RUSH TOWN THAT BEAT THE ODDS

D·E·R·M·O·T C·O·L·E

EPICENTER PRESS

FAIRBANKS • SEATTLE

Epicenter Press, Inc., is a regional press founded in Alaska whose interests include but are not limited to the arts, history, environment, and diverse cultures and lifestyles of the North Pacific and high latitudes. We seek both the traditional and innovative in publishing high-quality nonfiction tradebooks, contemporary art and photography giftbooks, and destination travel guides emphasizing Alaska, Washington, Oregon, and California.

Cover Photo: Children and adults parade through Fairbanks streets celebrating the news that the U.S. Senate approved Alaskan statehood on the last day of June 1958.

Editor: J. Stephen Lay
Cover and inside design: Elizabeth Watson
Proofreader: Lois Kelly
Maps: L. W. Nelson
Printer: Transcontinental Printing, Inc.
Text © 1999 by Dermot Cole

Library of Congress Catalog Card Number 99-072500

Printed in CANADA
First printing, April 1999
10 9 8 7 6 5 4 3 2

To order single copies of this title, mail $14.95 (WA residents add $1.29 state sales tax) plus $5 for priority-mail shipping to: Epicenter Press, Box 82368, Kenmore, WA 98028-0368.

Booksellers: Retail discounts are available from our distributor, Graphic Arts Center Publishing Co., Box 10306, Portland, OR 97210. Phone 800-452-3032.

This book is dedicated to my wife Debbie,
for the love and encouragement and patience that she
has shown with me for more than 20 years, and
to the memory of Don Carter, a great newspaperman
and a better friend.

Table of Contents

UAF Archives

Miners at the Union Mining Company pause for a photograph next to the sluice.

Foreword

When my identical twin brother Dermot asked me to write the foreword to his new book, I was both pleased and flattered. Finally I can use a favorite line that I once read in a book co-authored by Bernard and Marvin Kalb on the foreign policy of Henry Kissinger. "Needless to say," the Kalbs warned, "all of the mistakes in this book are my brother's."

Dermot is one of the hardest-working writers I have ever known and an ideal choice to write this new centennial history of Fairbanks. For nearly a quarter-century he has been a reporter and editor with the *Fairbanks Daily News-Miner*. During that time I guess he has written more than a couple of million words about life and times in the Tanana Valley. Politics, sports, crime, local government, education, he has covered them all. In the pages of the *News-Miner* he has written the equivalent of a book a year on Fairbanks since 1976. But beyond his prodigious newspaper work, he has also written three other historical volumes: *Frank Barr* (1986), a biography of an Alaskan bush pilot; *Hard Driving* (1991), a history of the 1908 auto race from New York to Paris; and *Amazing Pipeline Stories* (1997), a social history of the Trans-Alaska Pipeline.

Among his thousands of newspaper columns over the years, one of my favorites included a lovely Christmas parable from Heywood Broun, a story about a man's struggle to be at peace in the world, to hear once more "the voice of the herald angels." A good writer captures ideas and emotions we all recognize, and can help us, at least once in a while, to hear the angels sing.

Many subscribers have told me that Dermot's daily newspaper column is the first thing they read every day at breakfast. He and I have literally been mistaken for each other since the day we were born, so I can't begin to count how many times I've been praised for the fine column he wrote that morning. Often I try to explain, but usually I just say thanks, and think how lucky I am to get credit for a day's work that I didn't do. Of course I've sometimes felt the brunt of his critics. On one occasion a skeptical parking lot attendant would not let me leave the airport until I showed him my driver's license to prove I wasn't the guy who worked at the newspaper.

No modern journalist in Alaskan history has written so long—or so well—about Fairbanks, the humble little city that sprawls along the banks of the Chena. I think Dermot's only rival in that regard is the legendary W.F. "Wrong Font" Thompson, editor of the *News-Miner* from 1909 to 1925. Thompson's mantra, "Ain't God Good to Fairbanks" (perhaps sometimes a question and sometimes a statement of fact), symbolized the hope and faith a writer needs to keep producing day after day, year after year, recording history as it happens.

It is natural for a newspaperman to feel an affinity for the past, as reporters actually create the raw material of history. Though a newspaper is next to worthless when the news is no longer new, eventually the passage of time will make it valuable once again. Today's newspaper will be tomorrow's trash, but the day after tomorrow it will become a valued artifact. Nathaniel Hawthorne believed that old newspapers were talking ghosts. He delighted that "the rough and hurried paragraphs of these newspapers can recall the past so magically."

"With hasty pens," Hawthorne said of the newspaper fraternity, "they write for immortality."

For those who enjoy Dermot's newspaper column, this excursion into Fairbanks history, this look at the ghosts of Fairbanks, will be an extended treat. He begins with the early history of Fairbanks, a town born of high expectations and low water, and follows its history through the boom and bust of gold mining, world war, Cold War, and Trans-Alaska Pipeline. Through extensive research in the back files of Fairbanks newspapers and the holdings of the University of Alaska Archives, he has uncovered a wealth of original stories, and skillfully recounts more well- known tales in a fresh new way.

If you have lived in Alaska any length of time, this book is sure to bring back some forgotten memories. And if you are a more recent arrival, you are about to meet some of the quirky characters that have made the history of Fairbanks, Alaska, rich indeed.

In the years to come I expect I'll hear from many readers about how much they have enjoyed this latest book that I didn't write. Thanks for the kind words.

Terrence M. Cole, Professor of History
University of Alaska Fairbanks

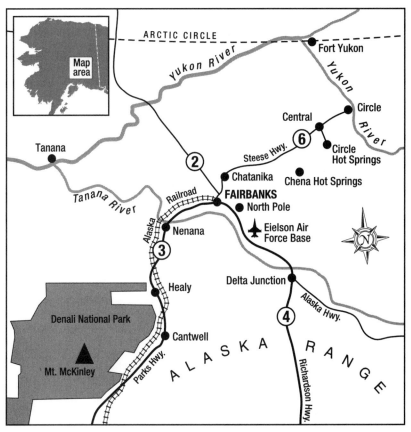

ARCTIC CIRCLE

Fort Yukon

Yukon River

Map area

Yukon River

Circle

Central

Tanana

Steese Hwy. ⑥

Circle Hot Springs

② Chatanika

Chena Hot Springs

Tanana River

Railroad

FAIRBANKS

North Pole

Alaska

Nenana

Eielson Air Force Base

③

N

Denali National Park

Healy

Delta Junction

Alaska Hwy.

④

Mt. McKinley

Cantwell

A L A S K A   R A N G E

Parks Hwy.

Richardson Hwy.

L. W. Nelson

11

Low Water and High Hopes

Candy Waugaman Collection

Gold, grubbed from the frozen soil, drew men to Fairbanks.

"Below us, far and wide, lay the glorious valley we had come to help settle. We sped down the long southern slope, through a beautiful forest of silver birch, out upon a flat plain, over a slough, across an island, through a heavy forest of spruce, and, from the north bank of the Chena River, the new Metropolis of the Tanana came into view on the opposite shore."

Judge James Wickersham,
April 1903

It was a modest metropolis that traced its origins to low water in the Chena River. In 1901, E.T. Barnette had hired the steamer *Lavelle Young* because he wanted to establish a trading post along the trail from Valdez to Eagle on the Tanana River, far upstream of where Fairbanks is today. Barnette spent $20,000 on a shipment of food, tools, other mer-

13

chandise, a dog team, and a horse. Joining him on the supply mission were his wife Isabelle, his partner, Charles Smith, and three other men.

The *Lavelle Young* churned upstream that August on the Chena River, trying to bypass a long stretch of shallow rapids on the Tanana River. But the riverboat ran aground on the Chena, and the owner, Captain Charles Adams, would go no farther upstream.

He argued for an hour with Barnette, but would only agree to take him about six miles downstream to a heavily wooded bank. Barnette wanted to go to the mouth of the Chena River, where George Belt and Nathan Hendricks had established a trading post, but the captain refused. Belt and Hendricks, whose post grew into the town of Chena, traded with Indians and hoped to supply the builders of the new military telegraph line that followed the Tanana River. Barnette figured that he'd be better off encamped at the mouth of the Chena, but the riverboat captain wouldn't take the chance of descending the river with a heavy load. His $6,000 contract with Barnette stated clearly that the provisions would be unloaded when the sternwheeler could no longer go upstream.

Because the riverboat did not have steam winches, traveling downstream with a full load in shallow water would increase the odds of getting stuck and being held fast by the current. The season was getting late, and Adams wanted to get back down the Yukon River.

At 4 p.m. on Aug. 26, 1901, near what is now the center of downtown Fairbanks, Adams had the $20,000 cargo unloaded on the riverbank. Deckhand Angus McDougall cut the first tree on shore, as men cleared a space to pile food, clothing, and equipment and set up tents.

As the *Lavelle Young* belched smoke and departed the next day, E.T. and Isabelle Barnette made no attempt to put on a false front.

"Mrs. Barnette was crying when we left the next day, as it did not look good to her either," Adams recalled. "Capt. Barnette was quite angry with me because I would not take him to the mouth of the slough." Barnette's stockpile would have remained on the banks of the Chena only temporarily, but for the arrival of two prospectors who were scouring the hills looking for gold—Felix Pedro and Tom Gilmore.

Pedro was a determined Italian immigrant who had hunted gold in

UAF Archives

Mining gold was physically demanding work with the payoff coming from the sluice box.

the Klondike and in Alaska for several years. As the *Lavelle Young* tried to ascend the Chena, Pedro spotted it from a hilltop, later commenting that the "greatest thrill of my life" was seeing the white smoke curling up from the steamer in the river. Pedro and Gilmore had run out of other food and were subsisting on game and berries, so they were anxious to buy from Barnette. They stocked up on flour, bacon, and beans and returned to the hills to continue searching for gold.

Barnette temporarily established a trading post on the riverbank, an outpost he first called "Chenoa City." He still had visions of transferring the entire load the next year to his ultimate destination of Tanana Crossing, on the trail between Valdez and Eagle, but he had no choice for the moment but to stay put.

A year later Pedro brought the news that would make the accidental trading post a permanent settlement; the prospector had found gold about 12 miles from Barnette's headquarters. Pedro staked the first claims on four creeks, he told his friends of what he had found, and they staked claims on Pedro, Cleary, Gold, and Twin Creeks. Before winter, speculators staked about 110 claims on nearly two dozen creeks, relying more on guesswork and wishful thinking than groundwork.

Barnette abandoned his plans to leave and decided to cash in on the gold strike by starting a town on the spot where he had been so unceremoniously deposited the preceding summer.

In selecting the name "Fairbanks," Barnette acted on the suggestion of Judge James Wickersham, one of the most powerful government officials in all of Alaska. Wickersham considered Senator Charles Fairbanks of Indiana his mentor and thought that a town named for the Republican power broker would be a fitting tribute. Though little remembered today, Fairbanks later served as vice president under Teddy Roosevelt.

In a huge region with no legislature and a governor with few powers, Wickersham's word was law in the Third Judicial District. Wickersham, age forty-five, a Republican from Tacoma, had been appointed a judge by President McKinley in 1900. In the years that followed he became one of the dominant figures in Alaska, an early proponent of Alaska statehood and a delegate to Congress for fourteen years.

Wickersham had said that he would help Barnette in whatever way he could to boost the town. Wickersham made good on his pledge when he moved his courthouse to Fairbanks, putting an official stamp of approval on the new town, which brought a good share of government business.

There was no assurance that the new mining camp would be another Klondike or Nome, but Barnette promoted it as such from the start. He became the town's first mayor and its first postmaster. He used his political and business connections to amass a fortune in Alaska over the next decade. But his tenure in Fairbanks would be marked by turmoil. When people in Fairbanks discovered some years later that Barnette, as a 24-year-old, had been jailed in Oregon in 1887 for larceny and had been banished from the state, his reputation took a beating—so did the customers at his bank. He left Alaska in disgrace about a decade after the founding of Fairbanks, with many blaming him for the demise of the Washington-Alaska Bank in 1911 and a $1 million loss to depositors.

Barnette faced embezzlement charges, but a Valdez jury convicted him of only one misdemeanor. The court of public opinion rendered a different verdict. For many years after he fled Fairbanks, the Fairbanks *Daily News-Miner* would refer to the act of robbing banks or stealing money as "Barnetting."

In the years before his name became a verb, Barnette demonstrated that he was a man of action, not afraid to brag or boast to attract people and money to his town. The embryonic promotion of Fairbanks, as undertaken by Barnette, included glowing letters to prospectors and people in high places, a salted mine, and other schemes designed to create a stampede to the middle of nowhere. With the skill of a veteran storyteller, Barnette embellished tales about the wealth waiting to be found in Fairbanks. "We have the best camp on the American side today," he proclaimed in one letter, describing the results of a new mining operation on Pedro Creek as "the best thing I ever saw."

He made it sound like Fairbanks was a sure bet, though a year later the first geologist who examined the area said, "Sufficient work has not yet been done to give definite information in regard to the average value and distribution of the pay dirt."

Barnette's most infamous act of exaggeration was his decision to send Jujiro Wada, a hardy dog musher and soldier of fortune, to spread the news of the Tanana bonanza in Dawson. Wada reached Dawson in January and gave glowing reports of the riches waiting in the Tanana Valley. The headline "RICH STRIKE MADE IN THE TANANA" greeted the readers of the *Yukon Sun* on Jan. 17, 1903, touching off a midwinter stam-

Chena, the town at the mouth of the river of the same name, rivaled Fairbanks for a few years, but later faded into obscurity when Fairbanks won the support of Federal Judge Wickersham.

pede in frigid temperatures. "Seven months from now," Wada told a reporter in Dawson, "all the lower river boats will run up the Tanana, for surely there is a second Klondike in that country."

Estimates of the number of people who made the trek for the second Klondike that winter ranged from several hundred to a thousand or more. They came from Rampart, Tanana, Nome, Circle, Valdez, and Dawson. Their enthusiasm was short-lived, however, as the stampeders discovered that almost no mining was going on, that the creeks had been tied up by mining speculators, and there was no work and no money in Barnette's Klondike.

"There wasn't anything here, but there were people coming on account of the strike that they'd heard about," said Ben Falls, one of the early arrivals. "Hundreds of people came along and they'd pitch tents and then they'd start to build themselves a cabin."

Many of the stampeders stayed at Chena, the settlement at the mouth of the Chena River that grew into a town and rivaled Fairbanks for a few years. An early account compared the fighting between Chena and Fairbanks to the rivalries of Tacoma and Seattle or St. Paul and Minneapolis.

George Smith, who championed the cause of Chena, often told his friends how he cut down as many trees as he could in the river, hoping to create gravel bars that would impede navigation to Fairbanks, a journey that was often a chancy proposition because of low water. In Fairbanks, Chena was subjected to ridicule. At one of the first social events ever held in Fairbanks, lawyer J.C. Kellum sang The Song of the Salmon, to the tune of "There'll Be a Hot Time in the Old Town Tonight."

It went, in part, "For they think they can outwit us and make us come to them, but to hell with their opinion for we do not care a damn, for this is the place the miners come. And we've got little Chena on the run. And if we don't beat them let Johnny get his gun. For we've got a hot time in Fairbanks tonight, Oh Chena!"

Trader Nathan Hendricks, testifying before Congress in 1903, said that "all sorts of characters" came in the first rush to Chena and they had "no respect for other people's rights.

"There were men who had located in this town who left town temporarily to go to the diggings. On their return their property was confiscated and they were kept out of their own buildings by Winchesters. There was no civil authority there at that time," he said. "We had no law providing for any temporary organization by the citizens to establish temporary regulations." A.S. Kirkpatrick staked a lot and pitched some tents for warehouses. He returned from a timber-hunting trip to find an empty lot with no tents.

In one respect, Chena was a better spot for a town because steamboats could always reach it in the summer; the Chena River's shallow water proved a hindrance to Fairbanks from the start. But Fairbanks had the political support of Wickersham, which turned out to be more important than geography or hydrology. In Fairbanks, lots could be had for the staking, plus a recording fee of $2.50. Frank Cleary, Barnette's brother-in-law, drew a map and designated city blocks. The first two streets were named, at Wickersham's suggestion, after members of Congress who were allies of the judge, John Lacey of Iowa and Francis Cushman of Tacoma.

Wickersham arrived in Fairbanks to get his first look at the new town, which had everything but gold, in April 1903. "A rough log structure, with spread-eagle wings looked liked a disreputable pig sty, but was in fact, Barnette's trading post, the only mercantile establishment in the new camp," Wickersham wrote. "A hundred yards up the stream, also facing the river, a half-finished two-story log building without doors or windows bore the homemade sign on a white cloth, 'Fairbanks Hotel.' Two other small log cabins marked, 'Pioneer,' and 'Northern,' made known to miners with wilderness thirst that civilization and its vices were there."

Wickersham named a deputy recorder to register mining claims and he staked a lot for the courthouse and approved plans for a jail. A few weeks later he published the mining camp's first newspaper, which at $5 for each of its six copies, was the most expensive in the world. It was also the only one that defended its editorial position by saying, "If you don't like our style, fly your kite, and produce your 30-30."

A lawyer from Circle, Abe Spring, castigated most of the early boomers as "ladies and gentlemen of leisure" and "a horde of non-producers, fellows the Canadian government were driving out of Dawson." Spring said they knew nothing about mining and had no interest in work, simply wanting to be on hand when the gold cleanup began in the spring. But because there were no more than a dozen men doing any mining, there was no big payoff in the spring of 1903 and most people left just as impulsively as they had come.

"As the season gradually advanced and little dust made its appearance in town, a spirit of unrest settled over the town," a 1904 account in *The Tanana Gold Fields* recounted.

A mass exodus began in late winter, when dog team travel was still possible, and increased when the rivers opened for navigation in the spring of 1903. "They all built rafts to go down river in the spring and some of them got back over the trail to Circle," prospector Falls said. "Just as fast as they came, they went back. If I'd have been older than I was, I might have stayed around Fairbanks, just to get in some stakes on the ground. But when everybody was leaving it didn't look very good to me, so I went prospecting that summer."

When it became apparent that the mining bonanza described by Wada didn't exist, angry miners held a meeting at which some demanded the lynching of the Japanese adventurer and Barnette. Harry Badger, one of the early arrivals from Dawson who stayed in Fairbanks, presided over the miners' meeting. "He went to trial all right and he was pretty near scared to death," Badger said of Wada. "I really don't think that they intended to lynch him. I think they intended to scare him and they did."

Along with the gold shortage, Fairbanks faced a food shortage. Gus Conradt said Barnette doubled his flour price because supplies were short. Barnette also tried to strong-arm the stampeders into buying his stocks of canned cabbage, canned spinach, and canned beets if they wanted some of his three-ton supply of flour.

"If you bought a 50-lb. sack of flour you had to take three cases of canned goods that weren't fit to eat," said Badger. During one tense moment Barnette posted a dozen men inside his trading post with 30-30 rifles to ward off trouble. Before there was any violence, however, Barnette reduced his flour prices and dropped the requirement that buyers purchase his canned goods.

"A lot of the fellows didn't have the price anyway, so we decided that Cap (Barnette) had better sell his flour one sack at a time and without any strings attached," Badger recalled.

According to one estimate, only about 100 people remained in Fairbanks by June 1903. Mining claims could be purchased for $50 and cabins for $25. There were vacant cabins and few people in the deserted mud tracks called Cushman and Lacey streets. This was the first, but not the last time in the history of Fairbanks that the community mood swung radically from extreme optimism to extreme pessimism. The departing prospectors had nothing good to say about the prospects for Barnette's fledgling town.

"Leading commercial companies who contemplated establishing trading posts backed out, with the result that, when the few who had faith in this camp were ready in the fall of 1903 to buy and pay new gold for their outfits for the following winter, neither food nor supplies nor tools were to be had for love or money," Spring wrote.

The muddy Fairbanks riverfront was already a busy place in June 1904 as stampeders used it as a stopping point on their way to the gold-rich creeks.

The gold strikes that would produce a second and more lasting stampede began in the fall. Not long afterward, Badger opened a real estate office in Fairbanks and started selling cabins that stampeders had unloaded only a couple of months before. "When someone would come in and want to stake a lot, I'd sell him one with a cabin already on it," Badger said.

Gold had been discovered, but it would take money and machinery to make it pay. The gold was deep in the ground, and it was hard work to dig tunnels to get to bedrock. There were no easy pickings as there had been at Nome in 1900 when thousands made fortunes on the beaches.

The miners recovered about $40,000 in gold that first summer, but food was in such short supply that if it hadn't been for an abundance of rabbits and healthy moose and caribou populations, there would have been a severe food shortage in the fall and winter. The Northern Commercial Co., which had bought Barnette's trading post and would remain a dominant force in Fairbanks for seventy years, advertised that its winter supply of flour, bacon, rice, ham, and potatoes was sold out by September.

"I have examined the stock of the Northern Commercial Co. and verified the above statement. All persons who are without provisions for the winter, would do well to make their arrangements before the last boat leaves," said Edgar Wickersham, deputy marshal of Fairbanks and brother of James Wickersham. At one point Edgar sent a telegram to Eagle warning that "People are leaving the camp on account of the shortage in grub. No grub to be had. Please notify everyone coming in that they must bring their own supplies."

The news from the NC Co. produced a run on the store, one that reminded people of the desperate situation during a food shortage in Dawson six years earlier. The remaining supplies of cornmeal and rolled oats sold within days, leaving only some potatoes, onions, sugar, lard, Worcestershire sauce, pepper, and dried fruit. Meals at Fairbanks restaurants jumped to $1.50 and the price of bread rose to 50 cents a loaf, before disappearing entirely.

That fall in the hungry camp the voters created the City of Fairbanks and chose the first city council. Barnette, the second-highest vote-getter, finagled his way into the mayor's chair. In one of his first official acts, he wrote Congress asking that food supplies at Fort Gibbon, the Army post on the Yukon River, be made available for sale in Fairbanks. He said between 2,000 and 2,500 people had moved to Fairbanks, but only 1,000 had provisions for the winter. "Extreme care should be taken that the vultures who speculate in human necessities should have no chance to fatten on the government liberality," Barnette wrote.

The war department allowed the sale of extra food, but there were critics in Fairbanks who claimed that Barnette was a bit of a vulture himself and that he had food stashed away, awaiting the day when he could sell it at a higher price.

A young Scotsman named George Preston arrived in Fairbanks on Jan. 4, 1904, about six weeks after leaving Valdez. "I thought for a while that we had, so to speak, 'jumped from the frying pan into the fire,' because Fairbanks at that date was not much of a town." He said the business section consisted of a few saloons, the NC Co. store, and a smaller store, all lit by kerosene lamps and candles.

After a hard winter on Fairbanks Creek, Preston returned to Fairbanks and became the NC Co. assistant bookkeeper. He stuck with the company until 1947, when he retired, at age seventy, as store manager. Preston remembered that when he first went to work at the

UAF Archives

Riverboats connected Fairbanks with the outside world, bringing food, equipment, and a steady stream of men hoping to find their fortunes in the interior Alaska river town.

NC Co. the shelves were almost bare and food supplies had to be rationed. "I recall we had one item—two or three sacks of frosted potatoes in the cellar. One of my first orders from Mr. Turner was that these potatoes were only to be sold in five pound lots and then only to men who had been suffering from scurvy during the winter."

It took time to eradicate the commercial skepticism about Fairbanks, but the town developed into a major gold mining center over the next year. ■

Boom Times on the Chena

"Miners Cavalcade bringing over a quarter of a million dollars gold dust from the creeks. Fairbanks May 20, 1905," reads the caption on this early post card.

Gold-seeking prospectors crowded the sternwheeler bound for Fairbanks. "You are in luck if you find space for your blanket on a secluded spot on the deck," geologist Sidney Paige wrote of his 1904 journey. "But all are gay and hopeful, and dreams of a farm in southern California, with an orange grove about the house, or a brownstone front on

25

Fifth Avenue in the East put energy into the weary."

The false start that marked the beginning of Fairbanks was history by 1904, when gold production began to soar. The population doubled and doubled again. Gold production reached $40,000 in 1903, $600,000 in 1904, $6 million in 1905 and $9 million in 1906. By 1910, nearly $30 million had been produced from Cleary, Ester, and Fairbanks Creeks, almost two-thirds of the gold mined in the region.

"Fairbanks is a thriving town of some two thousand souls and growing," Paige wrote. "In fact, it grows as you watch it, and it grows as you give up the watching and turn for a few moments of sleep. It has not yet, and it is to be hoped never will, bear the name of city, so often ill applied in the northern camps, where each collection of log cabins is dignified by that addition to the name of the first prospector who struck pay."

Paige counted ten saloons on the main street, all of them as busy as the drug stores, banks, and commercial stores. Merchants offered everything from rolls of wallpaper to polished oak dining tables at big city prices. "He that imagines that luxury does not exist in our far northern camps would need settle but one small bill for furnishing to become entirely convinced of the luxury of all things, even a sack of flour," the geologist wrote.

Merchants complained that shipping costs to Fairbanks made up more than half the purchase price. Once in Fairbanks, the local roads made deliveries difficult and further increased the cost. The first map of the Fairbanks area had the words "BIG SWAMP" and "No Bottom. Cannot Cross this flat in summer" on the land to the north and west of the city.

"There are chuck holes that a mule could drown in and there are slips and slides that could break the leg of a saw horse," one critic said.

Even finding the roads to the creeks challenged the traveler. A bridge on temporary pilings crossed the Chena. It was temporary because the ice took out the bridge every year, an event that marked the official start of spring.

"Someone may tell you to follow the telephone line, as it is straight," Paige wrote in 1904, about how best to reach the gold mines north of Fairbanks. "It is straight enough, one of the few straight things in the country, in fact, and the walking is good when you get

The Tanana Mines Railroad, later the Tanana Valley Railroad, served the mining camps with trains running on 45 miles of track from Chena to Chatanika.

down to it, but it's a long ways down and you must need make special efforts to extract each separate foot."

Local transportation gained more secure footing when construction began on the Tanana Mines Railway in 1905. Later known as the Tanana Valley Railroad, the rail line soon made it practical to bring in heavy boilers and other equipment to Fox, Cleary, Chatanika, Olnes, Gilmore, Vault, and the other mining camps along its 45 miles of track.

Falcon Joslin, president and founder of the line, raised $400,000 to buy out the London firm that helped finance the project, signing up new investors from New York, Chicago, and Boston. The cheapest things on the railroad when it was constructed were the locally cut spruce railroad ties, which cost thirty cents apiece.

A passenger on Joslin's train could see the men working on claims, hoisting buckets of gravel on hand-powered windlasses, and dumping them into flumes where the water washed the gravel from the gold. More prosperous miners used steam-powered windlasses and larger boilers, fueled by wood cut on nearby hillsides. One critic said the trains "whirled" passengers over the countryside at four miles per hour. With all the stops considered, the average train whirled along at ten miles per hour.

The vast wealth produced in the mines supported the operation of the narrow-gauge railroad and the development of Fairbanks, a town where lumber and beer ranked as the two major locally manufactured products. Two lumber mills worked at peak production to supply the town's building needs and the mining camps, while the Barthel Brewing Co. turned out "a beer with no bad after effects, the kind of beer that builds up the system."

"It is much healthier as a beverage than a beer that must be highly charged in order to stand the trip in from the Outside," said one connoisseur. Other signs of civilization appeared as well.

Enough families with children moved to Fairbanks that the town needed a school almost from the start. The first school had opened in 1903 with thirteen students and one teacher. Fees from city licenses paid for school operations, but the money ran out that winter and the school closed. A new school opened in 1904 with fifty students at homemade desks and tables. They found books in such short supply that three students might be seen sharing a geography book or a grammar book at the same time.

A larger school opened in 1907, a two-story affair with a distinctive cupola on top, that provided a clear view of the Alaska Range to the south. By late 1907, 150 pupils attended the school. Other families enrolled children in schools across the Chena River in Graehl and Garden Island, which were separate communities, and in mining camps such as Chena, Cleary, and Fox. At the Cleary school, the three coldest winter months were set aside for vacation; classes met throughout the summer.

The city had a telephone system that soon connected 314

Students learned their three R's at the Fairbanks Public School, which had two main floors and a cupola that stood at the pinnacle of early-day education in Fairbanks.

subscribers in Fairbanks and the surrounding mining camps. A 20-mile long-distance call to Cleary or one of the other creeks cost $2.50 for five minutes.

The Fairbanks business district featured three jewelry stores, a public school, barber shops, five churches, bath houses, hotels, cigar stores, butcher shops, and clothing stores, piped water, two hospitals operated by churches, and wooden sidewalks that expanded year by year.

The Eagles and various other fraternal organizations and clubs, including the Masons, the Arctic Brotherhood, the Odd Fellows, the Bohemians, and the Century Club enlivened the social scene. The Tanana Club looked out over First Avenue, the waterfront, and the industries on Garden Island. The club quarters featured leather chairs, electric lights, steam heat, a reading area with magazines and newspapers, a billiard room, a buffet, and a private card room. Business leaders belonged to the club and those who lived on the creeks maintained memberships as the club served as their headquarters in town.

At the dedication of the Eagles Hall in 1906, two men rode stationary bikes in what a witness called "the only indoor bicycle race ever indulged in the North, and the event was just as exciting as if the race had taken place on a track." They rode two miles in four minutes and two seconds, the crowd watching dials that showed how far they pedaled.

The idea of calling this up-and-coming town "Alaska's Golden Heart" became popular after Judge James Wickersham used the term during the ceremonies surrounding the driving of the golden spike for the Tanana Mines Railway in 1905. The Fairbanks Commercial Club adopted the slogan "Fairbanks, Alaska's Golden Heart. There's a Soft Spot in it for You" in 1911 and the club issued 125,000 golden heart stickers. "It is safe to say there is not a state in the union or a civilized country which has not been reached by some of them," the club claimed.

The club organized the first fairs in Fairbanks, planned Fourth of July and Arbor Day celebrations, bought fireworks for New Year's Eve, lobbied for development of a road to Chena Hot Springs, and promoted a variety of special events.

In a town with healthy beer, stationary bike racing, and a soft spot in its heart, there was an ordinance prohibiting the building of signs over the wooden sidewalks and the muddy city streets, with one glaring exception. Electric signs that could double as street lights did not fall under the prohibition because electric lights generated a warm glow that made Fairbanks feel more cheerful on long winter nights. Plus, the cash-strapped city didn't have to pay for the electricity.

One of the first big electric signs advertised the Tanana Saloon on First Avenue. Owner George Butler had a marquee that flashed the word "Tanana" then went dark before the letters would light up one by one. The cycle repeated every eight seconds, making the Tanana the most conspicuous place on the street. "Electricity has taken such a part in the business affairs of the world that no man in conducting an establishment of his own feels as if he has really kept pace with the world unless he has some electrical display," the *Fairbanks Times* reported Sept. 16, 1906. "No man who happened to look up First Avenue could help but see the ever-changing sign of that popular resort."

UAF Archives

A crowd gathered outside the Washington-Alaska Bank, one of three banks operating in Fairbanks in its first decade, to witness the transfer of a gold delivered for outlying creeks.

Those who walked along in the glare of the Tanana sign had come from all over the world, seeking adventure and a chance to strike it rich— miners, gamblers, camp followers, old soldiers, prizefighters, drifters, and family men, some with wives and children. The prosperity brought by gold kept three banks in the gold business. "Gold dust didn't have a chance to do much milling around as it had in Dawson, because the Fairbanks banks were active bidders for all the dust arriving in town," newspaperman Roy Southworth remembered. "In fact, they employed gold dust buyers who combed the creeks, bidding against each other for cleanups on the various creeks."

The banks encouraged depositors to take out checking accounts, he said. When depositors demanded cash, the banks would offer them gold coins, which were heavier than most people wanted to carry, thus the boom in bank accounts. The poor management of the original Fairbanks bank, owned by E.T. Barnette, and the nationwide financial panic of 1907, led at one point to the issuance of bank scrip for use as money. When placed upon a wet bartop, the thin money printed in Fairbanks would almost disintegrate before the glasses were empty. Some people spent the homemade bills with abandon, never quite believing their face value.

Missionary Hudson Stuck said that Dawson had been "largely depopulated" in 1904 by "the rush to Fairbanks of tradesmen and liquor dealers, caterers, and gamblers, and the male and female parasites of the miners, as well as by the miners and prospectors themselves."

Attorney John Clark said the saloons and dance halls occupied the most conspicuous places in the new town, creating the false impression that Fairbanks boasted more saloons than all other businesses combined. A man could find a drink for a quarter, and a gambler could find plenty of action.

"Gambling was wide open and games were running night and day in practically all of the saloons. To one who sought excitement and had the money to lose, the choice was various. The rattle of the ball and the call of the operator called many to the roulette wheel, while others had a system by which they believed they could overcome the dealer's percentage at faro. The crap table attracted those who desired noise with

The nuggets and flakes of gold fulfilled the dreams of men who worked hundreds of claims near Fairbanks in what became Alaska's richest mining district.

their recreation, while the less venturesome preferred black jack."

Clark said mine owners made the most daring gamblers, acting as if the gold boom would last forever. Clark estimated that not more than 1 in 500 men carried a gun and while there were occasional fisticuffs, he never witnessed a gunfight.

"The men who were here at that time were the pick of the world physically," Clark said. "I have seen crowds in dance halls at night where out of the perhaps 400 men, fully 60 percent were 6 feet and more in height and strong in proportion."

Gambling earned an unofficial blessing from the authorities, much the same as prostitution did, with the operators paying "fines" that helped run city government.

"For a time the gamblers on their own volition gave a few dollars each to the Chief of Police, but there was no warrant therefore in law and gambling was never recognized by the federal government," News-Miner editor W.F. Thompson said of those times. He said gambling "could have been stopped at any time during its career by the least of the inhabitants of Fairbanks, upon complaint."

Eventually the wide-open gambling operations were curbed, but the community attitude toward prostitution remained ambivalent for decades. In 1906 a grand jury reported that a city police officer had temporarily lived with a prostitute on the Fourth Avenue Line, the restricted district set up for prostitution. "When the evidence was not considered sufficient to justify an indictment for unlawful cohabitation, it was the general sense of the grand jury that the officer named was guilty of gross misconduct altogether unbefitting one whose duty it is to uphold the law and we therefore recommend to you his dismissal from the force," the grand jury wrote to the city council.

The council took up the matter, but allowed the officer to keep his job. There were those who saw nothing wrong with prostitution and gambling in a frontier town far from civilization. There were also people who defended the "social evil" as a necessity in a camp with so many unattached young men. It was easy to police the problem and keep it under control in a restricted district, readily visible to all visitors who saw the board fence on Fourth Avenue. In 1909 a federal investigator was shocked to find that Fairbanksans were "extremely friendly" toward prostitutes "to such an extent that the majority of the permanent residents know the prostitutes by their first and second names."

It did not sit well with everyone, however. Alonzo Maxey was a Fairbanksan who traveled to Washington to testify before Congress, voicing many complaints about government authorities in Alaska. He said the existence of the prostitution district proved that the people in charge of Fairbanks lacked a sense of propriety.

Maxey, who felt authorities had cheated him, said the leaders of Fairbanks tolerated gambling in the back of cigar stores, men at the telegraph stations resold goods they had purchased at subsidized prices, and jurors sometimes went drinking with defendants. In his litany of complaints, he included the tolerance for the Fairbanks Line. "There is a high board fence which faces on two of the principal cross streets," Maxey told the House Committee on the Territories on April 19, 1912. "Behind this fence, which is so conspicuous, is where the sporting element are kept, as they are called. They are corralled the same as cattle. It is the Fairbanks Zoological Park, established by James Wickersham, Delegate from Alaska, when he was a United States judge, a dispenser of justice, supposed to uphold the law as to protect the people. Now these people are simply advertised by the corral, and every school child knows what is behind that fence, and every woman.

"Talk about your wonders of Alaska," he said. "These women are human. There are men of the same class in the town, but they have votes and run at large. These women may be the sisters of someone, but they are down so they are being kicked. Now they are said to be a necessary evil. Well, a man goes down behind this fence. Someone in a town like Fairbanks will most likely know it. His women folks will most likely hear of it. Maybe a mother, a sister, a daughter, or in some instances, a wife. What do you imagine is a woman's feeling when told of some of her men having been seen going to the 'zoo'?"

He admitted that the people of Fairbanks "have not complained of this place," which was why it continued. Despite Maxey's claim, there's no proof that Wickersham, then delegate to Congress and a member of the committee, was the "father" of the Line. Fairbanks leaders either supported the line or regarded it as a necessary evil, which is why it continued in operation until the early 1950s.

Pioneer Clara Rust wrote that the city granted permission for the Line to operate, but it was understood that prostitutes would not solicit in the saloons or cafes or attend social functions. "Many of the cribs were owned by 'respectable' businessmen," Rust said. Over the years reformers launched numerous attempts to do away with the Line, but having prostitutes dispersed through the town created more problems. As the *News-Miner* put it after the boards temporarily came down before World War I, "the dispersal of the women has resulted in much disorder" and the streets they had moved to "are unsafe for decent women to use at night."

There were two towns within one, pioneer Margaret Murie wrote many years later. The women who went to church and had families couldn't speak to the women of the Line, but "there was a good deal of live-and-let-live, a good deal of gossip, but of a rather humorous, casual, unmalicious kind." ∎

Keeping Food on the Table

When she arrived in Fairbanks in 1904, Ida Crook discovered that she had to be resourceful to keep her children clothed and fed. It was impossible to buy children's clothes; the stores only had goods for men and women. "That winter I had my real experience in the North. We ran out of coal oil and candles, could not find any in the market for sale. The only light I had was grease in a saucer in which I placed a wick. I also had to make everything my boys wore right down to their foot wear. I made moccasins out of moose hide, since our stores carried nothing for children," she said.

As the mining camp boomed, stores began to carry a wide assortment of supplies, but many challenges remained. Serving meals was complicated due to a limited supply of local vegetables. The supply line stretched thousands of miles and was limited to the summer. Canned foods were a big part of menus and the empties often ended up in the river, which irritated the riverboat men. It was said that a treasure chest could be created from the tin cans that were thrown in the river, filled with silt, and threatened river navigation. "Who said there was no tin in Alaska? More tin has been imported thither than has been produced in the mines," mining engineer T.A. Rickard wrote in 1908.

Before the Alaska Railroad, people ordered staples a year ahead of time, stocking up on canned milk, referred to as the "canned cow," tomatoes, peas, corn, dried fruits, flour, sugar, beans, split peas, and cereals. It required advance planning. Keeping food edible for months required special handling. Before electrical refrigeration, Fairbanksans perfected practical techniques for food preservation. Most owned their own homes, which were usually small wood-heated cabins with low ceilings. A typical cabin had a root cellar reached by a trap door in the floor. The hole provided year-round refrigeration. When electric refrigerators became popular, some old-timers regarded them as a frill. With a root cellar in the summer and a back porch in the winter, who needed a refrigerator? "Electric refrigeration seems to be so unnecessary, but the new people have been used to it and they don't want a trap door in their kitchens and to lift it every time they want to put food away," one resident said in the 1930s.

Potatoes, turnips, carrots, celery, and other garden items could be stored for months in the root cellars. The dependable winter cold, which lasted from October to early April, made a natural deep freeze. Foods could be kept for an entire winter on the back porch or in a backyard cache. This provided a way to keep caribou, moose, or other game. A 1916 report noted the hunting limit was two moose, three caribou, and three sheep. There were no limits on squirrels, rabbits, geese, and ducks. Fresh meat arrived through periodic cattle drives over the trail from Valdez or Circle. Traders also delivered meat in storage containers shipped aboard steamboats. Some of the meat, one Fairbanksan remembered, "had the appearance of having been dug out of an Egyptian tomb, thoroughly embalmed and black with age."

Another advantage of the natural deep freeze was that cooked foods could be prepared in large batches and stored outside. Before meals, the cook would grab a loaf of bread or a pie to bring inside to warm up. Soup could be cooked in a big pot and divided into several portions, which, after freezing, would be broken off. Each spring, people harvested ice from the Chena River and stored the blocks under sawdust for cooling summer foods.

Eggs required delicate treatment. Residents bought cases of eggs in late summer and drew down the supply, periodically turning the eggs so they wouldn't spoil. Unlike people, eggs grew stronger with age. "But there was not much complaining about that situation," newspaper editor Roy Southworth once wrote. "As a matter of fact, the growing old process was so gradual in the cool of storage basements that no one realized how really strong they had become until early summer brought shipment of fresh eggs to town. And by that time everyone had become so used to the old eggs that the new ones seemed tasteless." It was a cardinal rule to break each egg separately so that when a bad one was discovered it did not ruin the rest. When airplane service was routine, customers would ask, "Are these air eggs?" as opposed to train eggs, over-the-trail eggs, or storage eggs. The arrival of the first boat of the season—always one of the most exciting moments of the year—brought with it mail as well as live chickens to replenish the egg supply. "The fresh eggs seemed a bit tasteless but mother really liked them," pioneer Dorothy Loftus once said. ■

Golden Days in Fairbanks

Miners worked underground during the winter when the gravel was frozen. The gravel removed during the winter was taken to the top, where gold could be removed during the spring thaw.

The first miners in Fairbanks had to do more than scratch the surface. The image of a prospector making it rich by bending over a stream bed with a gold pan in hand was as far from the truth as the story about the streets being paved with gold. A prospector might find signs of the precious metal on the ground, but the real treasure was often 100 feet down on the ancient rocks where the creek waters ran millions of years ago. The prospectors often had to dig deep to discover if they had a bonanza or a bust.

At first, the miners had only wood fires to thaw the ground. When the ashes cooled and the smoke cleared, they shoveled thawed ground and hauled it to the surface so another fire could be lit to continue the thawing cycle. Soon, wood-fired boilers provided the energy to melt the ground. The miners stripped the hillsides for fuel as they thawed and shoveled their way through subterranean expeditions, cutting passageways beneath millions of tons of dirt. Within a few years 600 boilers worked the creeks, burning immense quantities of 30-inch firewood. These were durable devices; many were made in Fairbanks machine shops and designed to be broken down into pieces and carried by dog teams, sleighs, or on pack horses.

The vertical shafts through the frozen ground were typically about eight feet square and lined with timbers. The shaft depth depended on the depth of the bedrock, where the gold was deposited eons ago.

At Chatanika men burrowed one shaft that extended down 315 feet, or more than 30 stories, but most shafts ranged from 20 feet to 180 feet beneath Dome, Pedro, Vault, Little Eldorado, Engineer, Goldstream, and other creeks. Cleary Creek, reputed to be the richest in Alaska, had so many tunnels that at one time it was said that a man could walk three miles underground from Chatanika to Cleary City.

In the winter it may have been forty below on the surface, but miners worked in temperatures close to freezing below ground, digging out gold-rich gravels from the tunnels that branched out from the bottom of the shafts. The gravel would be hoisted to the surface by hand or with steam-powered winches and collected in huge cone-shaped piles called "winter dumps." When running water returned with the spring thaw, the gravel could be washed to collect the gold in long, spindly sluice boxes.

It took considerable work to tunnel to bedrock, but the creeks outside of Fairbanks were rich enough to make it pay. "The miners who hunt for these paystreaks have courage and faith in the country," Bill Stiles wrote in 1908. "Not every hole sunk to bedrock strikes the pay. Newspapers seldom report the story of barren shafts and disappointed hopes, but the men who have stayed by the work and kept on sinking holes have usually been rewarded."

The work was as difficult as digging coal in Appalachia or digging ditches in

By 1910, Fairbanks had transformed from a rough mining town into a small city as seen in this photograph taken from the top of the newly built wireless station tower.

New York City. "My start was at Goldstream running a wheelbarrow in the drift, 10 hours a day for $5 a day and board," pioneer W.A. Coghill recalled of his first job in Fairbanks after arriving in 1908. "After two days I was ready to quit as it was no work for me. But, being the only one working there who could speak English, the foreman encouraged me to stay on so I assisted him with the points for a time, though not for long."

The miners wrestled No. 2 shovels and wheelbarrows in the dimly lit steam-filled tunnels, constantly watching for falling rocks. Hunks of the gravel ceiling would thaw and fall off, though usually the pieces were no more than forty pounds. At night the men drove hollow steel pipes from six to sixteen feet long into the frozen ground at the end of the tunnels. Long rubber hoses carried steam from the wood-fired boilers on the surface into the steel pipes. Miners removed the pipes ten hours later after the steam thawed the surrounding soil. Then they shoveled gold-rich dirt into wheelbarrows and hauled it to the bottom of the shaft, so it could be raised to the surface.

Mining engineer T.A. Rickard described what it was like to go down a seventy-foot shaft at the peak of the Fairbanks mining boom. "We went underground, standing erect on the edge of the bucket and holding the steel rope, while being lowered to the bottom of the shaft," Rickard wrote. "Lighting the candles offered by the manager, we walked along the boarded way over which the wheelbarrows pass. Being warned of their approach, we stepped to one side with our backs against the side of the level, while the procession of six men trundling wheelbarrows proceeded toward the shaft."

They wheeled 375-pound loads through underground air that felt like a cold-storage chamber. The men handling the wheelbarrows had to keep up with the leadman, who worked as quickly as he could, moving along the tunnel at a dogtrot with his backbreaking load. Each man hauled from 80 to 100 wheelbarrow loads, or six to seven cubic yards, of gravel per day. The tunnels that branched out from the main shaft, barely tall enough for a six-foot man, ran out 200 feet along the claim. Workers cut additional tunnels at right angles to create a honeycombed effect.

Leaseholders mined about three-quarters of the claims, paying the owners royalties of twenty-five to fifty percent. "Of the hundreds of rich owners in the district, only a few made a discovery of gold themselves, and only a few ever did any real work on their claims," Rickard wrote in 1909.

The workers went on strike in 1907, seeking a raise from $5 a day to $6 a day, plus room and board. "At the time of my visit it was nominally in force," Rickard said of the strike, "but the back of it was broken. After visiting the mines, seeing the conditions under which labor is performed, noting the character of the work and the system of ownership, operation, and exploitation, I found myself in sympathy with the laboring men," said Rickard, former state geologist of Colorado and editor of a mining magazine.

The underground tunnel work included many unusual hazards. One of the strangest happened to miner Bill McFadden in the winter of 1906, while digging gravel 170 feet below ground in a drift mine on Goldstream Creek, by candlelight. He heard a strange noise and was suddenly drenched as water flooded the tunnels and the shaft. The tunnel had apparently tapped into an underground stream.

He shot up like a projectile from a catapult, the freezing water pushing him toward the wintry daylight above. His partner at the surface didn't know what had happened, but he lowered a bucket into the shaft after hearing the noise. The bucket conked the desperate miner on the head when he was about fifteen feet below the surface, but McFadden grabbed the rope and his partner pulled him to safety.

"I thought I was a pretty fair swimmer," McFadden said later, "but I don't believe I ever made 150 feet in as fast time as it was made in that shaft. I think that will stand as a record for the air-swimming for many years to come. All I thought of was the fine new pick and shovel I forgot to grab when I left my day's work behind me."

The collective efforts of the men who mucked for gold in Fairbanks paid handsomely on the richest claims. The region exported millions in gold, much of it carried by pack train to Fairbanks banks. The banks had experts who could judge the relative worth of small pokes of gold dust on the spot. For quantities larger than $1,000, the usual method was to credit the miner's passbook at a value of $16 an ounce until the purity of the metal was established.

Assayers mixed the gold dust with borax and soda, which formed a chemical compound to remove impurities that usually showed up as black sand. The banks' blast furnaces, heated to 2,200 degrees, made molten gold that was poured into 50-ounce gold bars, each stamped with an identifying number.

One of the assayers, who had melted more than $50 million in gold in Dawson and Fairbanks, said he never thought of the value of what he handled. "I have been working in gold so long that the stuff seems to me just like corn or oats in the hands of a farmer," G.E. Beraud said.

The bankers weighed the bars and sent them by insured and registered mail, insured by Lloyds of London, to San Francisco or Seattle. Every mail shipment in the summer included gold as cargo, and about twice a month in the winter the horse-drawn stages carried shipments over the trail to Valdez, where they would be transferred to ships.

In a twelve-year period, the NC Co. stages carried $7 million of gold on the trail. "There were no guards and no firearms for the drivers but there was never a loss in express or passengers' belongings," L.D. Kitchener wrote in a history of the NC Co. "Wells Fargo found the service safer than that of earlier Western frontiers." ■

Dots and Dashes

After establishing military posts in Alaska, the United States Army received funds from Congress to build a telegraph system that carried the imposing name of the Washington Alaska Military Cable and Telegraph System, or WAMCATS, for short. Lt. William "Billy" Mitchell, who achieved notoriety decades later for his persistent advocacy of military air power, did his first work in Alaska on the ground, helping build the telegraph system.

One branch passed close by Fairbanks along the Tanana River, giving the mining camp a direct link with the outside world, albeit an expensive one. At first Fairbanks messages traveled over land lines to Eagle, which connected with a telegraph system in Canada. Later, an undersea cable from Valdez connected to the world beyond. In 1908, a wireless station, powered by a gasoline engine with one kilowatt of power, began transmitting telegraphs from Fairbanks. The 176-foot steel frame wireless station towered over everything in Fairbanks. An army officer overseeing the Fairbanks installation said it was the first time a wireless system had been used to send messages so far inland, 360 miles from the coast.

Candy Waugaman Collection

The wireless tower provided dependable communication with the rest of the world.

In 1916, a ten-word day message from Fairbanks to New York cost $4.85. At first, the telegraphers in Fairbanks wrote in pencil because the incoming signals were so faint the noise of the typewriters drowned out the Morse Code. They managed to increase the volume, but the high cost and limited capacity of the radiotelegraph restricted communication to official business, commercial messages, and emergency contacts. It was not a system for idle messages.

Trial by Fire

The NC Company dominated the waterfront in early Fairbanks. In a town built entirely of wood, fire was a constant threat. That threat was realized in May 1906.

When the great earthquake and fire struck San Francisco in April 1906, relief poured in from towns large and small. Bakers in Los Angeles donated 25,000 loaves a day. The Philadelphia Athletics sent their share of one day's gate receipts, $639.39, and the prosperous four-year-old gold mining camp of Fairbanks, Alaska raised $20,000, most of it in less than twenty-four hours.

A month later, the San Francisco Chamber of Commerce had reason

45

to ask if the devastated city by the bay could return the favor, for Fairbanks had suffered a calamity of its own. On the afternoon and evening of May 22, 1906, the bustling mining camp on the Chena River almost disappeared from the face of the earth. The response to the San Francisco offer was remembered later as something on the order of, "Thanks. No assistance needed. Somewhat disfigured, but still on the paystreak and have more money for the San Francisco sufferers if needed."

It had been a hot and dry spring. Miners on the creeks had been running gravel through sluice boxes and bringing a steady supply of gold dust to the banks. Every teller's window had lines that afternoon. A patient sat in the dentist's chair in the office of Dr. Moore in the Fairbanks Building on Cushman Street. R.J. Geis, one of the building owners, said later that the dentist used an alcohol light on his desk to heat his instruments before putting them into a patient's mouth to pull teeth. The dentist had his back turned when a breeze through the open window blew the curtain into the flame at about 4:30 p.m. The fabric became a flaming torch, and within seconds, fire engulfed the room. The patient and the dentist raced from the office and the cry of "Fire" rang through the heart of the mining camp.

"The flames spread so quickly that it was only a few minutes until the building, which was then a three-story structure, was a seething mass," wrote W.F. Thompson, editor of the *Fairbanks Daily News-Miner*. "Professional men in all parts of the building were compelled to jump from their windows to save their lives, and only through the greatest good fortune was there no serious accident."

Firemen and volunteers struggled to get the hand-drawn fire hose cart to the blaze, but they could do little to slow the fire.

"The fire fiend favored no one," the *Fairbanks Daily Times* reported the next day. "From the stately Fairbanks building to the little cabin of the secondhand dealer; all were wiped out. Nothing spared."

The city had only one team of horses in the fire department, a team used to pull a cart that sprayed a chemical on fires, but the chemical supply only lasted for a few minutes. The flames damaged the valves on the water mains, leaving little pressure to pump water into the buildings.

Attorney John Clark had an office in the Washington-Alaska Bank

Building, a structure connected on the second floor with the building where the fire began. Clark grabbed a newly repaired typewriter and a pile of valuable papers and raced downstairs, only to be met by flames in the stairwell. Someone had opened the iron door connecting the two buildings. "I lost my eyebrows, part of my hair, my typewriter, which I dropped in order to use my hands to protect my face, the papers which I abandoned for the same reason and in addition was scared out of several years growth," he wrote later.

Clark's partner, meanwhile, hurried about the office trying to save about $300,000 in promissory notes from Dawson. He stood in a window yelling for a ladder, displaying a "varied and lurid, sulfurous vocabulary." He threw down the papers, which were taken to the jail for safekeeping, but that was a wasted effort as the jail soon burned to the ground.

Clark's partner kept yelling for help from the window and would not jump. "He told the whole world what he thought of them and then centered his attention on the absent fire department, and, when he got started on that subject, he really did a wonderful piece of word painting, and even the paint on that side of the building where there was not as yet any fire shriveled up and showered down upon the sidewalk," Clark wrote.

At the Washington-Alaska Bank, employees and bystanders hurried to put valuable papers in the vault, while nearby at the Red Cross Drug Store men saved supplies from the flames. Every available team of horses hauled goods to safety from the stores in the fire's path. "Many were the teams worth a dollar a second that hauled goods for anybody and everybody and the owners would accept no remuneration," a reporter observed.

With the fire that day, hotel man William Waechter, owner of the Riverside Hotel, had been burned out four times in the north. Waechter also was in the cattle business and the loss of his uninsured hotel was offset somewhat by having recently sold $30,000 worth of cattle to Fairbanks stores. Like most of the other businessmen, he carried no insurance. "It is impossible to carry insurance either at Fairbanks or Dawson as the rates are prohibitive," Waechter told a Seattle reporter.

The Senate Saloon had a safe that had survived five fires in Dawson and Fairbanks. The safe had $2,200 in it when the fire struck, in addition to $17,000 in gold dust belonging to miners. When the ashes cooled, the outside of the safe was blackened, but the only damage inside was the drying out of the moose skin of the gold pokes.

Reporter Casey Moran, who had earned fame in Dawson for once writing a story on a slow news day about the discovery of Noah's Ark in Alaska, stationed himself in the telegraph office and sent news of the fire to the *Seattle Post-Intelligencer*, which reported the next day: "Fairbanks is in ruins. The entire business district has been burned to the ground. The loss is estimated at $2,000,000."

Men dynamited buildings trying to contain the fire and battled to keep the flames away from the Northern Commercial Co. warehouses that contained much of the Fairbanks food supply. Four steamers tied up alongside the waterfront docks directed streams of water on the sides and roof of the NC Co. Men drenched wool blankets and nailed them to the eaves to keep the flames from spreading.

According to company lore, NC Co. store manager Volney Richmond Sr., who also managed the company's power plant, ordered that the store's bacon supply be thrown into the boiler to build the water pressure. "At 500 pounds of bacon, the hot grease was a thunderous roar and pressure was rising," an NC Co. history said. "At 900 pounds of bacon, water was stronger in the hose lines and the volunteers could play their streams over men rushing in and out of the crackling buildings."

A ton of bacon was burned to a crisp and the extra pressure helped save the NC Co. warehouses, L. D. Kitchener wrote in a 1954 company history. It was not the only time that the company helped save Fairbanks' bacon. When a 1919 fire threatened the town, company crews burned 14 cords of specially dried wood, which was kept in reserve at the power plant for emergencies, and three crates of bacon to build more steam in the boiler and generate higher water pressure.

The day after the 1906 fire, the *Fairbanks News* ran a full-page ad from the NC Co. that contained only these words: "There are supplies enough in town for every one. Prices will not be raised. Northern Commercial Co."

By concentrating firefighting efforts at Turner Street, the NC Co. warehouses were saved, though the wood buildings were "heated almost to ignition." The fire burned all night, and for many hours, loud explosions came from the saloon cellars on First Avenue as liquor bottles and barrels blew up from the heat. The chief of police recruited fourteen new deputies and kept everyone out of the burned area except those with passes. The fire destroyed everything from First Avenue to Third Avenue and from Cushman to Lacey Street.

The gold boom was strong enough that there was never any doubt about rebuilding the town. The Washington-Alaska Bank was still in flames when the owners announced that they would open the next day at the regular time on the same spot. They missed that goal by thirty minutes. At the First National Bank across the street at Second and Cushman, a crew panned the ashes for lost gold.

The headlines in the *Fairbanks News* said, "Fire Can Not Stop Fairbanks" and "New and Better Town Arising from Smoking Ruins." The day after the fire the telegraph office took in nearly $700 as every merchant in town ordered new supplies from the states to replace what was destroyed. The business district was gone, but the four-fifths of the town that made up its residential area remained intact, as well as the largest store.

The Outlet Clothing Co. announced a "Genuine Fire Sale," while MacArthur's Drug Store advertised "Paper on the wall a little scorched but still doing business in the same old way." The C&C, otherwise known as Cloes & Cameron, advised "After a Hot Fire get a Cold Drink."

There was some confusion in the aftermath about goods that had been saved by volunteers. "George Butler has two cash registers somewhere in town, but he has not met the man who saved them," said one account. A merchant pointed out that "it's about time my friends were telling me where I can find the goods they mentioned as saving the evening of the fire."

That summer both Fairbanks sawmills seldom stopped buzzing as they turned out two million board feet of lumber for the rebuilding effort. Within a few months few signs of the fire remained, except some buildings had not been painted.

"Then gambling was in flower, the element of chance was abroad in the land and our recuperative powers were unnaturally great," Thompson wrote of the rapid rebound.

One court case that arose from the fire concerned an order for twenty-five cases of eggs stored in Barrett's warehouse. On the day of the fire, the firm of Tharp, Rusk & Smith signed the papers to buy the eggs for $500. Later that day the warehouse burned, destroying nineteen cases, though it appeared that some of the eggs cooked by the fire made it to the menu at Century Hall the day after. A jury ruled that Tharp, Rusk & Smith had to pay $500 because it owned the eggs and could have taken possession before the fire struck.

UAF Archives / Bunnell Collection

After the 1906 fire, the fire department had two teams of horses pulling fire carts.

Five new fire hydrants appeared that summer along with other fire safety measures. The city fire department bought 1,000 more feet of hose and rigged up a hose cart pulled by horses instead of men. The department also ordered more ladders and nozzle tips, but they didn't show up on the last steamer of the season. A new fire harness allowed the firemen to cut forty seconds off the time required to hook up the horses. Fire Chief Buckley said firemen could reduce the hitching time by eight more seconds by moving the fire station bunk room, so the fire pole would be nearer the horses' heads.

Walter Clark, a visiting Washington reporter and future Alaska governor, said the 1906 fire was a disaster, but a few months later he found it did "not have a very appreciable effect on the prosperity of the town. Some of the residents were obliged to borrow money to rebuild, but some of them have already paid off their indebtedness and the others will pull through unless the town has another setback such as can come only through fire or earthquake or some similar natural calamity."

"Fairbanks is one of the youngest towns on the map and it may not be too much to say that it is the largest town of its age, promoted and built up entirely by individual enterprise, anywhere in the world," Clark said. ■

The expansive premises of the NC Company, with departments catering to customers of all tastes, served Fairbanks for decades at its First Avenue location.

The Northern Commercial Co.

The Northern Commercial Co. planted the company flag in 1903 after buying Barnette's trading post. In that clearing in the wilderness, while prospectors built small cabins, the NC built an empire. It sold food, hardware, clothing, and operated a power plant with a sixty-foot smokestack, water system, and steam-heating system to serve the business center. By 1907, the NC grossed $2 million a year from its various enterprises. The company emerged as one of the biggest factors in the early development of Fairbanks because of its large supply of goods for sale and its policies of extending credit, which allowed many miners to develop their claims.

Critics called the company the "Octopus" because its tentacles spread in so many directions. It was a "mighty lucky thing for our camp and Our Town that the 'Octopus' had eight arms to wind about the camp and hold it firm, or most of us wouldn't be here," W.F. Thompson said in 1920. "To them the camp could look for protection from every evil—starvation, fire, darkness, and lack of transportation."

One businessman who liked to take issue with the Octopus was John O. Ellis, who fancied himself a regular business buccaneer. His shop was called "The Pirate Ship" and he had a marauding ship painted on his store sign. He often used his newspaper ads to poke fun at competitors, the government, the marshal, and others in high places. All of these were given as reasons for people to climb aboard and buy on the Pirate Ship downtown.

"The Octopus (Dad-bing 'em) have went and tcrn up our street again, to fix the water or steam pipes. And it don't look as though they know how to fix 'em or will ever get it done. In the meantime we are worrying about fire and our lack of fire protection until that street is closed again so we will start in and sell everything cheaper on The Pirate Ship," read a typical ad for Ellis. At the NC store miners could buy butter in one- or two-pound bricks as well as rice, beans, peas, and other dried foods. There was condensed milk and lots of "Canned P's." A 1912 ad listed the following under Canned P's: Parsnips, pumpkin, pearl onion, potatoes (sweet), pate de foie gras, pigs' feet, pork and beans, pickles, peppers, peaches, pears, plums, prunes, pineapples, pie fruit, preserves, plum pudding, and peanut butter. The company advertised as "Progressive Purveyors of Pure, Palatable Products."

The Octopus supplied more than heat, light, water, mining supplies, clothing, and food. It had a machine shop where skilled workmen made mining tools. The NC also operated, under a contract with Ed S. Orr & Co., the winter stage line to Valdez. The company kept a reserve wood supply in the power house for emergencies, guaranteeing that the boilers would always have fuel. The boilers roared through forty cords a day.

Meeting this demand provided employment to hundreds of men through the years to cut wood in an ever-expanding circle from Fairbanks and hauled it in on horse-drawn sleds with towering loads. A steel track ran from the power plant about ten blocks to the end of Barnette Street, where the company kept its stockpile of several thousand cords. Before the Alaska Railroad created an

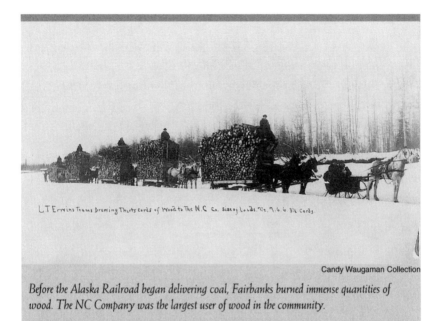

L.T. Erwins Teams Drawing Thirty cords of Wood to The N.C Co. Size of Loads. Vz. 7, 6, 6 3½ Cords.

Before the Alaska Railroad began delivering coal, Fairbanks burned immense quantities of wood. The NC Company was the largest user of wood in the community.

economical way to transport coal from the south, Fairbanks burned wood.

In many houses, the fires burned from November until April, with only brief respites when the chimney had to be cleaned of soot to prevent house fires. There were tracks outside in the snow around every cabin, leading from the woodpile to the front door. L.T. Erwin ran one of the largest woodcutting firms. A photograph of his "wood train" shows sled drivers riding twelve to fourteen feet above the ground on several cords of wood. By 1913, Fairbanks homes and businesses burned 12,000-14,000 cords each year, mainly birch and spruce cut within five to seven miles of the city. For several years people talked about what would happen when Fairbanks ran out of wood. The NC Co. bought 8,500 cords in 1913, making it the biggest of the wood burners.

"There is no danger of a wood famine in the Fairbanks district for some years to come," said George Coleman of the NC Co. "For the last two or three years people have been telling me that we were due to run out of wood. Many predicted that the fast depletion of the wooded side hills meant nothing but substitution of fuel for Fairbanks, but I, for one, think there is enough timber within a seven-mile radius of Fairbanks to supply the camp for at least three more years to come." ■

5

Town of Robinson Crusoes

Candy Waugaman Collection

Moose can be dangerous, but that didn't stop some Fairbanksans from treating them like pets.

From the close of navigation in October until river ice broke up the following spring, Fairbanks had little contact with the rest of the world. Horse-drawn stages made the week-long trip from Valdez and telegraph reports brought world events to the newspapers, but the towns-people lived largely in isolation.

"Geography is making of the people of the Tanana Valley a race of Robinson Crusoes. They are learning rapidly to live on their own resources and to provide their own needs," the *Fairbanks Times* reported in its 1910 *Industrial Edition.*

The census that year counted 3,541 people living in the city of muddy streets and wooden sidewalks, while thousands more inhabited the small mining camps nearby, many along the tracks of the Tanana Valley Railroad. In this isolated region, which had grown into the largest city in Alaska within a few years, the manager of the NC Co. found it advisable one fall to poll the people on whether the town should adopt its own time zone. He suggested shifting clocks forward an hour so the ever-decreasing daylight would last longer into the afternoon and evening. By a margin of four-to-one, however, Fairbanksans preferred leaving their clocks alone, and said the company whistle should keep sounding reveille at the same hour.

One of the regular weekly highlights occurred when the mail stage pulled into town, greeted by residents eager to see who might be on the stage and what the mail might bring. "It was a great sight to see the mail stage coming down Cushman Street, four head of horses with bells merrily jingling and Harry Martin of Tolovana holding the lines," said freighter William Coghill.

Cushman Street, which ran ten blocks through the center of the town, marked the end of the Valdez trail, and students in the school often made themselves eager witnesses when the stage came in, providing a tangible connection to the world Outside. A frequent Fairbanks passenger on the stage from Valdez recalled "how we enjoyed riding all day in that perfectly fresh invigorating air and at night going into the roadhouse, with its big wood fires, and the delicious smell of hot coffee and various foods finely cooked; also mixed with what was often a mixture called 'hot toddy,' mixed in the Southern style." She said for those who had taken the pledge to not drink alcohol, it was a great punishment to decline a roadhouse hot toddy. It was a thrill to go flying downhill "hitting the bumps and always uncertain as to just where you might land."

The stages were the only way to travel, but a man who was labeled an "automobile crank" by the newspapers announced plans to drive cars over the same trail. He said he could make the trip in a day with a car equipped with steel spikes on the tires. It would be several decades before the trip became a one-day journey, which is why the *Fairbanks News* editorialized that he was dreaming.

There was constant political pressure to improve the trail to Valdez, and Major Wilds Richardson, known as "Major Dick," led the early effort to upgrade the path to the sea.

For transportation, horses and dogs played a central role in the life of the town, but rarely as silent partners. When the city council took steps in 1906 to require that horses and cattle be prohibited from roaming free at night, resident James Plaistel praised the action, saying people shouldn't be made to suffer because horses wandered the streets at all hours. "The thing has come to be a nuisance of the first order and should be stopped. Not only do the horses keep up a constant clamor all night, but they break down fences and destroy flowers and garden beds. It should not be allowed in a town of this size."

Decibel for decibel, the horses had nothing on the canine population. At night, dogs would start to howl; a single barking dog could start a chain reaction that didn't stop until every dog joined. The NC whistle would also set them off. "It was hard on the newcomers," a resident said of the barking dogs, "but after a time one became so accustomed to it that, like the sound of the street cars to the city dwellers, it was only noticeable when it had ceased."

Another noisemaker, the automobile, began to appear early on. H.H. Ross drove a Pope-Toledo and a Franklin in 1906 on the muddy trails; the next year he added a Thomas Flyer to his fleet, delivering freight and passengers to the creeks. It was soon said that one of the prime advantages of an automobile was that it didn't need hay and oats three times a day or straw or sawdust for its bed at night.

"The local road system has been substantially complete this season by the construction of the road from Fairbanks to Gilmore and the improvement of the roads between Fairbanks and Ester and between Ester and Chena," wrote John Zug of the Alaska Road Commission in 1908.

Samson Hardware and the NC Co. both got into the automobile business at an early date. At one time the NC Co. sold both Ford and Dodge cars. Its hardware department display window was said to be the only one in Alaska large enough to in-

Robert "Bobby" Sheldon completed the first trip by automobile to Valdez from Fairbanks in 1913. Sheldon did more than anyone to promote the automobile in the rugged country.

clude a complete car with all the tools and extra equipment.

Local automobile owners who perhaps felt a bit defensive about the complaints of pedestrians and sharing the streets, even offered a fake set of rules of the road in 1909. The regulations said pedestrians needed licenses and had to wear "a white light in front and a red light in the rear."

By 1914 Fairbanks had twenty-five automobiles; thirteen had arrived the previous year. These included seven Model T's, one Cadillac, one Pierce-Arrow, and sixteen other models. Bobby Sheldon was the first to drive south to Valdez over the twelve-foot-wide trail, while a three-quarter-ton Army truck made the first northbound journey to Fairbanks. The Army truck averaged eight to nine miles per hour, but on the best sections of road it hit speeds of eighteen miles per hour on that 1913 journey. Sheldon, who had looked at car pictures in magazines, but had never actually seen a car, built his first one as a boy in Skagway by putting a tiny gas engine on a buckboard. He did more than anyone to promote the use of the automobile over tough terrain. He adorned his Ford with a placard promising "Valdez or Bust."

Sheldon operated the "Sheldon Auto Stage" over what he called the "All-American" route with "no international complications," to Valdez. It cost $100 to go to Valdez with forty pounds of baggage free.

The road to Valdez remained a rough one for many years. A traveler in 1917, Carlton Fitehett, said it was "too bad we had neglected to provide our car with a scow and paddle wheel. Later on, when the car dropped out of sight and was submerged in mud, I decided that what we needed most was a periscope and a compass to steer by while traveling beneath the surface of the Sea of Muck."

Transportation to the Interior of Alaska had always been tough and calls for a railroad to the coast that would help pull Fairbanks out of the mud and end its isolation began soon after the town got started. "At the present time many of the residents, especially the women folks, feel that they are prisoners, as they can only go and come during the short summer season of open navigation," said L.A. Nadeau in 1906. "Naturally it makes them all the more restless to get Outside occasionally, but once you make it possible for them to go any time of the year, many of them would not care to go so often and better still, they would consider this their home, their real home and plan accordingly."

Nadeau, the former general agent for the Northern Pacific Railroad in Seattle, predicted a railroad would change the psychology of life in Fairbanks and invigorate mining. "Not only will the cost of living be cheaper to the miner, but he will be able to get his heavy machinery at a price low enough to enable him to work a vast quantity of low-grade ground, which cannot be touched under present conditions," he said.

Eight years later, as historian Edwin Fitch put it, "a faith in railroads combined with a lack of faith in railroad personalities" led Congress to appropriate $35 million to build the Alaska Railroad. The residents of Fairbanks, convinced that this action signaled a new ear of prosperity, staged a big celebration on Feb. 23, 1914.

For that night only, women walked into and out of saloons. Saloon keeper Bill McPhee said, "Ladies who visit The Washington tonight will be as safe as though they were in God's vest pocket." The California Saloon announced, "We have the largest and Airiest Saloon in Town and Ladies desiring to see the saloons of Fairbanks as they are will find perfect protection." Many women dressed as men entered the saloons, their identities hidden by masks. Even the prostitutes on the Fourth Avenue Line joined in the festivities. One observer said later the prostitutes who participated in the masquerade "were the most ladylike of all those who took part in the dancing and general merrymaking."

Writing about himself and the rest of the town, a bleary-eyed W.F. Thompson asked the next day: "Why is it that an old, gray-headed man with one foot in the grave and the other in discard, will get out on occasion such as yesterday, swallow a gallon or two of various poisons and cavort like a fool yearling calf, storing up aches and pains that will last him for a week, and otherwise make a bally ass of himself? It passeth understanding, yet they WILL do it, even as you and I."

The Shriners' yell for the day was, "Delegate Wickersham's; Chamberlain's too; And Woodrow Wilson's Choo! Choo! Choo!; Fairbanks Terminal—that will do, Zip! Zip! Boom!"

There was hope that the railroad would make all the difference in the world, providing better communication and cheaper transportation of supplies. "Upon the selection of Fairbanks as the site of the Interior terminal of the government railroad depends greatness for the capital of that great valley," Governor John Strong said in August 1915. ■

The George C. Thomas Library at the corner of First Avenue and Cowles Street was kept open for many years through the efforts of local women's and church organizations.

Open Door Policy

"What do you want of a key?" a landlord once asked a new arrival to Fairbanks. In early-day Fairbanks, many houses didn't have locks. The open-door policy extended to the George C. Thomas Memorial Library, the stately structure at First and Cowles built with funds provided by Thomas, a Philadelphian who had read that the miners didn't have a good place to read and smoke.

For many years the circulating department was open set hours at the library, where fiction was far more popular than nonfiction, but the rest of the building never closed. It was a challenge to keep the library going through the decades and there were times when its survival seemed questionable, but it withstood crisis after crisis, staffed by women connected to civic clubs and others from St. Matthew's Episcopal Church.

For $1 and a promise to retain it as a library forever, the city bought the building in 1942. The library became a borough department in the 1960s and a long-standing campaign for a new and larger public library came to fruition in the late 1970s. The old Thomas library building, which looks about the same as it did when it was built, is now in private hands. ■

A Unique Ordinance

Even a moose is subject to the law of the land. At least that's what the
Fairbanks mayor and city council decided in 1913 when a bartender's pet
moose became too much of a bother. The ordinance gained such notoriety
that you can still find books that claim Fairbanks is the only place in the
world where it is against the law for a moose to use city sidewalks.

Pete Buckholtz, a bartender in Bill McPhee's saloon, which occupied the site
where the Lacey Street Theater now stands. Buckholtz had acquired a calf moose
from hunters. "The animal became very tame and would follow either Pete or me,"
Charles Schiek recalled. "The moose had been broken to harness and could be
hitched to a sled. In winter he was fed on potatoes and stale bread and sometimes
either Pete or I would go into the woods, then nearby, and cut some willow for
the creature. I remember he wouldn't eat rolled oats."

The moose had "gained in docility and affection" when Mayor Andrew
Nerland decided that something had to be done. The moose followed
Buckholtz and, like him, made its headquarters in McPhee's saloon.
Buckholtz had been asked many times to keep the moose out of the saloon,
but he refused. City officials could not prohibit possession of a live moose,
but there was a city sidewalk in front of the saloon and the city fathers could
ban moose from city sidewalks. The moose was the only one in Fairbanks
and the ordinance was designed to keep him out of the saloon.

The Associated Press distributed the moose tale, and it continues to
be mentioned today by writers who mistakenly assume that it is still in
effect. If a moose is spotted on a sidewalk in this day and age, bystanders
give it a wide berth because a moose is a dangerous animal, but the
police will not accuse it of trespassing.

Twenty-five years after the moose ordinance, the city approved a ban
on keeping wolves and coyotes because of the danger to children. "Civilization has caught up with us," firewood dealer "Honest" Ike Thompson said in
1940. "There were no bans on moose, bears, wolves, or coyotes, and timber
was so plentiful it had to be felled for cabin space when I first settled here.

"Maybe I ought to move on. I won't. As long as I have my health,
nothing else matters." ■

6

End of the Glory Days

UAF Archives

*Riverboats crowd the docks on the Chena River in downtown Fairbanks. In the summer
everything moved via the river route.*

Falcon Joslin, who built the narrow gauge railroad that helped spur
the early development of Fairbanks, took a back seat to no one in pre-
dicting a glittering future for the boom town. But even Joslin had doubts.
He knew that to every mining camp there is a season and that the season
for Fairbanks may have passed. "There is a terrible spirit of depression
here," Joslin wrote his wife in 1909, when gold mining was at an all-time
high. "It is the sense that the camp is over and will decline fast. I hardly

63

think it will go down so very quickly, but go down surely it will and perhaps just drop all at once. It seems everybody is trying to get away."

In the years that followed, gold mining declined, and it often seemed that everybody did try to get away, starting a long decline for what had been Alaska's largest town. Gold production dropped by half in two years and kept falling.

"The first to suffer from the decreased placer output of the district are the small merchants; for the number of business houses in operation in the old days is still maintained with little reduction, and the population is insufficient at present to warrant the continued existence of all of them," writer Philip Knowlton said in 1916.

Fairbanks recorded thirty-six deaths and twenty-one births that year and almost any place in town could be bought for less than it had cost to build. In 1918, gold production was ten percent of what it had been nine years earlier. Wartime inflation and the fixed price of gold combined to nearly wipe out the mining industry. Excess goods piled up in the stores, and merchants trimmed their orders. "There were empty cabins all over town, inhabited only by mud swallows nesting under the eaves," pioneer Clara Rust wrote.

James Wickersham, Alaska's delegate to Congress, hoped to fight the decline with a plan to create a college in Fairbanks. According to legend, Wickersham picked up a book used as a doorstop in his office one day and he stumbled over the section that allowed land grant colleges an annual federal payment of $50,000. Wickersham ignored his colleagues' derision, and his bill to start the college won approval at 4 a.m. on March 4, 1915, the last act of the Sixty-Third Congress. Before the territorial Legislature had a chance to formally approve the college plan, Wickersham starting building college spirit by dedicating a cornerstone on July 4, 1915 at the then-non-existent institution. He chose a site on a tree-covered ridge about four-and-a-half miles out of Fairbanks on the road to the agricultural experiment station for the Alaska Agricultural College and School of Mines. Wickersham acknowledged privately that he acted "without authority of law" in dedicating the cornerstone. But the old block of concrete occupies a central spot on the University of Alaska Fairbanks campus today, a testament to Wickersham's determination.

UAF Archives / Bunnell Collection

A large crowd gathered for the 1922 dedication of the Alaska Agricultural College and School of Mines. On the first day of classes there were six faculty members to teach the six students.

He had also played a key role in winning approval of the legislation to create the Alaska Railroad, a plan sponsored by those who wanted to "open up" the country and attract new settlers. In addition to dedicating the college cornerstone that July, Wickersham also conducted what has been described as the first formal discussion on land rights of Alaska's Native people. Though there was no established settlement at the exact site where Barnette founded Fairbanks more than a dozen years earlier, Athabaskan Indians had traveled through the area for thousands of years. They had camped on the Tanana and Chena Rivers and hunted game and fished. In fact, the very bluff chosen for the college site turned out to be an ancient camp used 3,000 years ago. The college archeological site in Fairbanks provided the first evidence supporting the theory that humans entered North America from Asia over the Bering Land Bridge.

In 1915, Wickersham met with the chiefs of seven Athabaskan villages in the Fairbanks library on First Avenue and warned that with the railroad, more white men would be coming to settle the land.

"White men are coming out and taking up the land," Wickersham said. "They are staking homesteads, cultivating the land, raising potatoes, and all kinds of crops."

The Indian chiefs asked that the government "not let the white people come near us. Let us live our own lives in the customs we know." But Wickersham said that change was coming with the railroad and he suggested the Indians seek 160-acre allotments or ask for the establishment of reservations to hold onto some of the land.

"We don't want to go on a reservation, but wish to stay perfectly free just as we are now and go about just the same as now," Chief Ivan said. Wickersham insisted that reservations held many advantages, but the chiefs were adamant. "I tell you that we are people on the go and I believe if we were put in one place, we would just die off like rabbits," Chief Alexander of Tolovana said. The tribal leaders said they wanted to be left alone and "to live here all the time."

The land pressures that Wickersham predicted would come with future population increases didn't happen overnight. It wasn't until World War II during the military buildup in Alaska that dramatic population growth began. Even so, the discussions on Native land claims would not come to the forefront as a political issue until Alaska became a state.

During that July in 1915 when Wickersham unveiled the cornerstone of the college and met with the Athabaskan Chiefs, some questioned whether Fairbanks might have a future at all because of its prolonged economic decline. It was even a hardship to keep St. Joseph's Hospital open. A fundraising campaign a few years later helped the hospital raise $2,200. "Knowing the present dull condition of the district, we feel that when so much money has gone from the Interior of Alaska to the Outside for all the splendid war work done by this district, the response to the local call has been extremely generous," the Sisters of Providence, operators of the hospital, wrote in a card of thanks.

News-Miner Editor W.F. Thompson had taken to looking back nostalgically in his shrinking newspaper, recalling the rise and fall of Fairbanks with its "floating" population of gamblers, dancehall queens, and prizefighters. "The games, girls, prizefighters, and easy-money guys were plentiful. They stopped prizefighting, but the fighters went back to the restaurant and dishwashing from which they had graduated. Then they killed gambling; remove the gambling from a camp and you remove the gamblers and their camp followers. The big operators worked out the richest of their ground and took the money to San Francisco; with the cessation of working mines most of the miners disappeared and a few went prospecting; only a small part of the mining population is of the prospecting class. Some gamblers went farming and prospecting and they are here yet. Farming has taken the place of gambling because it is such a game of chance."

Thompson figured that the Fairbanks area had lost 10,000 people between 1911 and 1923, dropping to about 1,000. Others said the 1,000 estimate was too generous. "We have enough homes for several times as many population as we have because the homes of the town were built to house 15,000 people, those leaving being unable to take their homes with them. There being so many unoccupied cabins and store buildings, real estate is cheaper than in any other town on earth," Thompson wrote.

The water system was hurting because the NC Co. didn't have enough customers to warrant burning wood to keep the lines unfrozen, the company complained in 1919. At this time the town had a look, one English visitor noted, of "unmerited hopelessness."

Charlotte Cameron said she occupied the grandest room in the Nordale Hotel, and that while it was not luxurious, she knew that it had been constructed rapidly and it was a wonder it was as good as it was. "I had a creaky bed, which must have supported many a heavy weight; the electric light was tied up to the bedstead by a man's well-worn necktie; a red Brussels carpet, very aged, had green cabbage roses sprawling all over it. The partitions, through which you could hear the slightest movement, were fashioned of thin boards, covered with canvas, and papered over." There was an electric bell to ring for the hotel's staff, but the wires to it were cut. She said that considering the long distance and the difficulty of travel, she could forgive the "dilapidated, inartistic surroundings and make the best of things."

Many of the young men of the camp had been drafted or gone to the States to look for work during World War I, which exacerbated the decline.

Fairbanks watched as its young, healthy men marched off to World War I after being drafted or volunteering. Many never returned. Some were killed. Others found opportunities elsewhere.

In April 1917, a couple of hours after Congress approved the Declaration of War against Germany, the men in Fairbanks met at the federal courtroom. "Hidebound pacifists" were declared unwelcome in the packed room of 150 businessmen and miners. All signed a pledge saying they would do what they could to support the war effort, gathering 100 more signatures within a couple of days. That was the start of the "Alaska Loyal League." Men began collecting donations from the crowd. They agreed to send a telegram to President Woodrow Wilson saying that Fairbanks was ready to do its part to make the world safe for democracy.

The men had buttons made that showed an American flag and wired the authorities for official suggestions on how they could be useful in the war. The *News-Miner* urged all foreign-born people to join the Loyal League because that would allay suspicions. "Nobody in Fairbanks knows and few suspect the danger there is to the United States at this time from internal disloyalty," a reporter wrote. Men would be needed to do "secret service work" and "ferret out all disloyal movements and expose them," while others would be called upon to raise money and work at home. "The potato raiser on Birch Hill, sowing and cultivating potatoes to add to the supply of the United States is no less a warrior than he who is fighting at the Front, for the fighter must eat to fight and the grower must be depended upon for the supplies to keep the army fighting."

The war of attrition that left 12 million dead or missing destroyed the notion that the physical isolation of Fairbanks somehow insulated the camp from the bloodiest war in history. "There was a time, not so very many years ago, when we were, along with the rest of you, all puffed up with pride at what we considered the sure-thing civilization of the then-world," Thompson wrote six months after the United States entered the war. "It seemed to us and we were prone to brag about it, that this little old world of ours had reached a place in time where we were several blocks ahead of all the ages in the matter of sense, discretion, judgment, and culture, and that we had long since passed the crossroads where human intelligence could return to brute struggle and human inventiveness to human destruction. Just then one bloodthirsty Alien stuck a knife into another bloodthirsty Alien and the whole world went mad."

In the wartime fervor, anything related to Germany became suspect. At the Red Cross drug store in Fairbanks, Frank Clark had a large supply of the popular "47-11" soap. When a woman came into his store and insisted on buying some, he said he'd have to sell her another brand. Clark said he'd rather take the soap and dump it in the Chena than sell it. When she asked why, Clark dug out a box and turned it over, where the words "Made in Strasburg, Germany" were printed. "I don't want that soap. I wouldn't have it in the house," she told him.

A middle-aged waitress who had been born in Germany but never naturalized as a U.S. citizen worried that she would be placed in an internment camp. She spread the word that she would pay $500 to any American citizen in Fairbanks who would marry her. Harry Slater, a saloon roustabout known as the Popcorn Kid, took her up on the offer and they were married at the Pioneer Hotel. After the wedding, Popcorn revealed that he hadn't become a naturalized citizen either. She left Fairbanks, leaving Popcorn without benefit of $500 or a wife.

Townsmen formed a local military unit called the Fairbanks Home Guard. Guard members patrolled in two-hour shifts at night to make sure the city was safe from subversive activity. Four guards marched on each shift in the city and two patrolled across the river on Garden Island, all armed with revolvers. The men guarded all warehouses, especially those containing food and government property. The Loyal League took a census of Fairbanks, getting all male residents to fill out a form that asked name, age, address, and numerous other questions about background and citizenship. People wrote if they could ride a horse, drive a car, handle a team of horses, understand telegraphy, swim, or operate steam engines.

There was ready sympathy for the men at the front in part because a growing number of friends and relatives joined the fight. Clifford Moody was the first person from Interior Alaska to register for the draft. "I like this Army stuff fine so far," Moody wrote a friend from South Carolina after he had been wearing the uniform for a time. "It sure is a healthy proposition as we get only the plainest kind of food, get plenty of exercise and sleep in the open (practically) all the time."

Fairbanks responded to SOS calls, meaning "Send Over Socks" or "Send Over Sweaters" and in the summer of 1918, Fairbanks knitters shipped 168 pairs of socks, 33 sweaters, 16 hospital shirts, and 4 handkerchiefs to help the doughboys in France.

The mail from the front was censored. A letter to R.C. Wood in black ink looked like kids had scribbled on it in purple because of all the censored remarks. Written from somewhere "on the front" in August 1918, Frank Wood said he had to wear his gas mask and helmet all day and that the steel helmet got so hot in the sun he couldn't put his hand on it.

The war death of B.W. Dunkel, the man for whom Dunkel Street is named, struck home with his friends in Fairbanks. An American citizen, he enlisted in the British Army in 1916 and had been sent to France. "I do not fear death in the least," he said in one of his last letters. "Why should I fear what is merely a transition from one sphere to another?"

One of the first four pupils to graduate from Fairbanks High School was Percy Thomas Joseph Blanchfield, known as "Old Brick," a boy with blond hair and freckles. While fighting in Europe, Blanchfield wrote a friend in Fairbanks, George Hering, about the "joys of soldiering in sunny France."

"They call it sunny because it only rains six days in the week, and the sun roasts you on the seventh. I am writing this letter at a time when I ought to be cleaning my clothes, which are covered with this delightful French mud. The mud here is a great friend. It will never desert you. It if wasn't for the mud and the insects, etc., I believe I would be lonely."

Like thousands of other soldiers on both sides, for Blanchfield the war amounted to life in the trenches. He watched as observation balloons were shelled by the Germans, forcing the occupants to dive out by parachutes from 1,000 feet up.

"Life here gets rather monotonous, as there is so much sameness. When we are in the line, it is exciting enough and no pleasure at any time, especially during wet weather, when there is a couple of feet of mud and water in the trenches," he wrote.

"Drop me a line if you have time and remember me as your old pal," he said, writing two weeks before his death. Blanchfield, for whom Blanchfield Alley would be named in downtown Fairbanks, was killed in action near Lens City and Hill 70 in France, while serving with the Canadian infantry.

On June 3, 1919, four trees were planted outside the Fairbanks school, dedicated to four former students who died while serving in the Army. The trees honored Blanchfield, Lawrence Morency, Dorman Baker, and Lawrence Auten. The school service flag bore fifty-two stars, representing former students who served; four were golden stars "for golden lives given to honor their alma mater and their country."

The Fairbanks students who gathered to plant the trees had all been involved with war preparations on the home front. All students had enrolled in the Junior Red Cross, bought war bonds and lobbied adults to do the same. They "adopted" an eleven-year-old French orphan, sent money to help other French orphans, grew "war gardens" during the summer, and collected tin foil and bottles. Norman Burglin, age twelve, saved $60 and was paying $2 a month for a war bond, earning the money by collecting and selling bottles and crates. "When I came to Fairbanks bottles were to be had everywhere, but now they are hard to find," he said.

Every child with $5 received an account at the First National Bank and a passbook. Within three months of starting this program, sixty stu-

Candy Waugaman Collection

Before the steel Cushman Street Bridge was built in 1917, the power of the spring breakup usually took out the supports for the temporary wooden bridges built every year.

dents had $950 on deposit. The students raised money to help the French orphans and wrote letters of encouragement. "I have a brother too," Lillian Lien wrote. "He is seven years old. He is in the first grade. I have a dog and some chickens." Lillian wrote of picking crocuses in the spring, blueberries in the summer, and how she liked to go on the swings, slide, merry-go-round, and seesaw outside the red schoolhouse.

The children of Fairbanks all signed a Loyalty Pledge under direction from the territory's Commissioner of Education and the school kept copies on file. In signing the Loyalty Pledge, students promised to be loyal to the United States and the Territory of Alaska, to help save wheat, meat, fats, and sugar; to not waste food or anything else useful to the country; to save sugar by cutting their candy consumption in half; to be

72

careful with shoes and clothing so that they could be worn for as long as possible; and to perform school tasks in a way to be useful to the country and the world. Most families gave up meat for one or two days a week and gave up wheat for one day a week, part of the national drive known as "Hooverizing," after Herbert Hoover, who led the campaign to cut food consumption so that there would be more to relieve hunger overseas. School lessons included a weekly Loyalty Hour in which the students discussed how they met the goals of the Loyalty Pledge. With the younger children, the teachers worked not only on patriotism and the three R's, but also on cleanliness.

"When every child in the second grade has perfectly clean hands and nails, they are awarded 'A' and the room can have a star. Owing to the carelessness of some boys, very few stars have been awarded this month, and the teacher is considering a black list if improvement is not made," the school report for April 1919 said.

Anita Nordale, secretary-treasurer of the class of 1919, served as platoon leader of the high school, as all children from grades five through twelve had military drills during the afternoon recess. "We who are not old enough to fight for our country are glad to do all we can at home, for even the children of Alaska want to keep up the reputation of our territory for loyalty and patriotism," she said.

One of the most joyous events during the long years of Fairbanks' decline happened on Nov. 11, 1918 when the NC whistle blew at 2 a.m., sounding the news that the war to end all wars had ended. Days before the official announcement came, the *News-Miner* warned Fairbanksans that when "the steam heat in all the stores falls and falls because of the steam that is trying to strangle that whistle," the people in Fairbanks would know that peace had come. "For once, that whistle will be music to our ears."

Within minutes every child in town was up and many of them joined their parents in a parade that lasted an hour, enlivened by cheering and the blowing and hammering of every noisemaker they could find. Most people went home then, but some stayed up all night, parading and shouting in the streets. Church bells rang and patriots fired their guns in the air.

Some of the youngest children repeated the refrain, "Kaiser Bill went up the hill to take a look at France; Kaiser Bill came down the hill with bullets in his pants." As soon as school began the next morning, the teachers realized they would never get the students settled, so a holiday was declared. The teachers formed a line with the kids and the parade snaked through the streets again, ending at Beam & Chamberlain's store, where the owners opened the candy case in honor of the victory.

At the official Peace Celebration that night, 600-700 people assembled for an all-night dance, which broke up with the orchestra playing "Home Sweet Home" at 5 a.m. Despite prohibition, the officers of the law looked the other way that night over the flagrant public use of "joy water," but warned that this was a onetime event occasioned by the universal relief at the end of hostilities. Then it was back to "Sober Street" and the end of public displays of drinking.

The war set back Fairbanks by ten years, Judge Cecil Clegg said, by slowing construction of the railroad and draining Fairbanks of its young men. With inflation, the original appropriation to build the railroad proved woefully inadequate, and the construction timetable stretched out to eight years. The $35 million was gone long before the railroad was finished as labor, materials, and equipment shot up in price. Congress provided additional appropriations of $30 million to continue the work. And what kept Fairbanks going? A man who returned to the town after seeking his fortune Outside said that those who stayed in Fairbanks "were the luckiest people on earth." He said everyone talked about the "desire to sell out and get out; where the hell would you go if you left here? Outside if you wish to buy a hoe and have the price to do so, you buy, and the taxes each year are more than enough to make the investment bad business."

During and after the war years, another enemy arose that was harder to fight than the Germans. The Spanish Flu epidemic that swept the world happened just as the young Alaskans had gone Outside to train for war. All but three of the seventy-seven Alaskans in Edby Davis' company sent to the States for training were hospitalized with the flu and seven men died. One of those who perished was Dorman Baker, for whom the Fairbanks American Legion post was later named. Hjalmar Nordale, one of the Fairbanks recruits who survived the 1918 flu, said the men he was with regarded Fort Dodge, Iowa as a "hell hole."

"These are dark days for B Company," he wrote to his parents in late 1918. "All but six squads were in the hospital with the flu at one time and 18 of our 180 have died. You seldom see a smile on our boys' faces now, and the chief pastime is hanging around the telephone waiting to hear who is the next victim.

"They told us that it was the old-fashioned Grippe, but it was not. It knocks the spots right out of a man. I had a fever of 104.6 and a high pulse and the funny part of it is that a person seems able to shake it off. It is now nearly 10 days since I first got it and I still feel all broken up; headaches just like father had last summer, just over the eyes and every time that I touch my head there I want to jump; nose all stopped up and a 'fancy cough.' IF THIS THING HITS FAIRBANKS and any of you feel the least bit sick, GO TO BED AND STAY THERE until your temperature has become normal for at least 24 hours."

The flu epidemic ravaged the world, killing 20 million people, and spread across the north in 1918-19, creating the worst disaster in Alaska's history. About 2,000-3,000 people died and 500 children, most of them Natives from remote villages, lost their parents. Health authorities set up quarantine areas for anyone coming into Interior Alaska. City officials demanded that the mails be fumigated and that passengers en route to Fairbanks wait at a quarantine station for five days before entering the town. It was nearly two years later, when the danger was thought to have passed, that a serious flu outbreak finally occurred in Fairbanks.

A Cordova newspaper reported that the epidemic "crippled every industry and business in Fairbanks. When the disease was at its height, whole families were stricken at the same time, leaving them absolutely helpless."

One of the volunteers who cared for the bedridden was writer Mary Lee Davis, who said that doctors and nurses found themselves unable to keep up with the hundreds who were seriously ill. According to one estimate about ninety percent of the population of Fairbanks was sick, "but there was no excitement, no fear and everyone turned in and helped everyone else," attorney John Clark stated. "As a result, out of over 1,300 cases, we only lost 9 and in those instances there were other causes than the flu that contributed to the death." ∎

Women's Suffrage and the Booze Bugler

The first bill adopted by the First Alaska Legislature didn't create a stir in Alaska, but it changed the shape of Alaska politics forever. The measure opened voting to women, who had been denied the right up until 1913. "I signed it without hesitation and quite naturally the passage of this progressive measure was hailed with delight by women's suffragist organizations everywhere," Governor Walter Clark said.

Two years later, Governor J.F.A. Strong said women's suffrage was an "unqualified success" in Alaska.

"The operation of the law has not besmirched the women of Alaska; it has not unsexed them nor caused them to take on 'unwomanly attributes' or unfitted them to become wives and mothers, or to attend to their domestic duties generally. And their votes, as a rule, are cast on the side of progress and morality. To the votes of the women of Alaska may be ascribed the crystallization of public sentiment against the liquor traffic in the Territory," the governor wrote Aug. 12, 1915 to the head of a New York organization working for women's suffrage in that state.

While there had been some talk that giving women the right to vote was a gimmick to make the shrinking Alaska population appear larger than it was by increasing the vote totals on Election Day, others said it was a true recognition that women had a role to play in public life.

In Faribanks, about 150 of the new voters attended an organizational meeting in 1914 as their baptism in politics. When the wife of a prominent Republican attorney asked the only man present to explain a ballot and how to mark an "X" next to a candidate's name, Mary Gibson, a college graduate, objected. "We don't want to bother with all that child play," she said, calling instead for a speech by a Socialist organizer on the history of the women's suffrage movement. Out of that meeting came the Fairbanks Women's Civic Club.

The campaign against "Demon Rum" in Alaska was in keeping with the national uproar that led to the 18th Amendment, which banned the manufacture and sale of alcohol. In Alaska, the supporters of the saloons

76

and breweries called for a temperate approach. In Fairbanks, Barthel's Beer was advertised as "The Drink of the Temperate."

Dubbed the "booze bugler" of Fairbanks by women leading the prohibition campaign, W.F. Thompson of the *News-Miner* argued that the problem with prohibition was that it didn't prohibit. "You can no more legislate morals and temperance into a people than you can legislate them into success," the bugler said. Such arguments didn't pass muster with the Women's Christian Temperance Union and the Anti-Saloon League, organizations whose idea of temperance was abstinence. The legislature agreed in 1915 to allow an advisory vote on prohibition, since it was a weak governing body unable to enact prohibition without approval from Congress. After a bitter campaign, the measure carried by a nearly two-to-one margin on Nov. 7, 1916, a vote of 9,052 "dry" and 4,835 "wet."

The next year Congress approved a "bone dry" bill for Alaska that became the law of the land, forcing the saloons and liquor dealers to close in 1918. New Year's Eve in 1917 in Fairbanks was the quietest in the camp's history, with the ban on liquor sales taking effect at midnight. "Not much excitement in evening," Edby Davis wrote in his diary.

In Fairbanks, the vote was 501 "dry" to 433 "wet," a closer tally than in many parts of Alaska. The only local neighborhood where the "wet" voters prevailed was Chena, where the count stood at 12-10. With the adoption of prohibition, saloon men either found new occupations or left Alaska. The Barthel Brewing Co. bought the Tanana Bottling Works and began brewing distilled water on a "Polar Still," selling "the purest water known to science," for $1 for a five-gallon can. The plant could turn out 250 gallons of the pure stuff every 10 hours. Just before prohibition became the law of the land, the NC Co. sold its liquor off to those who wanted to stock up, $5 for a gallon of rye and $3.50 for a gallon of rum or gin.

A poem about the coming of prohibition to Alaska written by an outsider offered one view of the new era: "The sourdough, when he wants a drink, will amble to the Yukon's brink, and quaff a horn of H-

2-O, a harmless drink, as well you know; then go his way in search of gold; and sing an ode to water cold, and when he makes a stake he'll go, to camp and buy a drink or so, of orangeade, near beer, or lime, and swear he's had a ripping time."

Thompson, who once said he had sampled every brand of intoxicant from Hostetter's Stomach Bitters to hard cider, claimed that the enforcement of the liquor ban in Fairbanks was one of the factors in the town's continued decline into the 1920s. The authorities did not go after the business and professional classes for prohibition violations, Thompson said in a 1925 letter, but they did go after the workingmen with the "spirit of witchhunting days."

One reporter estimated in 1919 that Fairbanksans had perhaps as many as a hundred small stills producing "a little liquid sunshine. The goods may be crudely made, and may not be as healthful as the properly manufactured joy water, but they have a kick in them and jar a feller loose from the impression than the hands of the world are raised against him." Thompson longed for what he called the "Morn of Reason" when alcohol would be legal again, but it didn't dawn until 1933, seven years after his death. ■

7

A Ghost Town No More

UAF Archives / Bunnell Collection

Many a gold nugget and thousands of pokes came from miners' sluice boxes before mining evolved from an industry controlled by individuals to capital-intensive enterprises of large companies.

The three dozen newspapermen and photographers who accompanied Warren G. Harding, the first United States president to visit Fairbanks, prepared for the worst. Rear Admiral Hugh Rodman had advised them of the rugged conditions in Alaska. "We bought heavy shirts and heavy underwear, sweaters and galoshes, and leggings to protect our shins against mosquitoes," said Charlie Ross, a reporter for the *St. Louis Post-Dispatch*.

Ross and the rest of the ink-stained wretches dressed for the big chill when they arrived in Fairbanks in 1923, as part of the ceremony to mark completion of the Alaska Railroad. It was not January, however, but the middle of July. "We reached Fairbanks that evening and paid a night visit under the midnight sun to the Alaska Agricultural College and Experiment station," Ross recalled twenty-five years later, when he served as President Harry Truman's press secretary. "The next day the President made a speech under the blazing sun at the baseball park. Three persons were prostrated by the 94 degree heat." Ross said the newspapermen and other "wearers of heavy underwear" threatened reprisals against Admiral Rodman. It's not known if the admiral followed his own advice about dressing for the weather, but he endured baked Alaska along with everyone else in the Harding party.

Harding had Secret Service protection on the trip, provided by two agents who worked with local law enforcement agencies. The only scare occurred in Nenana on the day Harding drove the golden spike. R.C. Morris of Nenana rushed to the rear platform of the railroad car where Harding and Alaska Governor Scott Bone were standing. The agents grabbed Morris because they thought he was trying to attack the president, but the governor intervened and assured them that Morris was simply giving a boisterous Nenana welcome.

The view by the visitors was something else. Almost every reporter, according to the *Seward Gateway*, "went out of his way to dip his pencil in wormwood and gall in describing the Alaskan Railroad and its effect upon the development of the country." The correspondents "probably thought we were a bunch of hicks," the Seward editor continued, but complaints of reporters notwithstanding, there was no denying that the rail line promised a new era for the Interior of Alaska.

"No one would have conjectured, when the project was entered upon, that the nation's chief executive would himself drive the last spike," Secretary of Interior Hubert Work said to the crowd at Nenana. "Mr. President, these steel bands you join will almost connect the Pacific Ocean with the Arctic Ocean through the Yukon." Work said the ceremony marked "the passing of the last frontier." Harding tapped the $600 golden spike gently with the hammer. Then it was removed and he took aim at an iron spike. "When the movie men immortalized the ceremony, the President strikes twice at the iron spike and misses it. He then sinks it, counting a four on the hole," Ross said, alluding to the sport that kept Harding out on the links with his clubs at least two afternoons a week back in Washington.

Harding was in Alaska, escaping the worries of Washington, D.C. scandals within his administration, on what was intended to be a two-month journey of 25,000 miles, the longest trip ever taken by an American president while in office. Accompanying him on the so-called "Voyage of Understanding" were his wife, three members of his cabinet, the Speaker of the House of Representatives, and other dignitaries.

Secretary of Commerce and future president Herbert Hoover was one of only five bridge players on the trip. Hoover wrote later that the president was increasingly nervous on the ship heading north and they took shifts playing bridge with Harding because the president wanted to play starting after breakfast and continuing until after midnight, only taking breaks for meals. "For some reason I developed a distaste for bridge on this journey and never played it again," Hoover recalled.

The bridge players put the cards away for a round of speeches and receptions in Seward and Anchorage, the railroad ceremony in Nenana, and the trip to Fairbanks. While in Fairbanks, Harding ate ripe tomatoes at Rickert's Farm, shook hands with just about everyone, attended a midnight banquet in the Model Cafe, a lunch at the Masonic Temple, and received the gift of a gold collar for his dog Laddie. He visited the *News-Miner*, where the former Ohio newspaper publisher set his initials in type. When he tried to wash the printer's ink off his hands, he "hollered," according to the *News-Miner*, that things weren't right because a clean towel was by the sink instead of one dirty enough to stand up on its own.

In his main speech at the Fairbanks ball park, where the children and adults wore their best clothes, Harding said that even people who had read a lot about Alaska pictured it as "the home of the itinerant adventurer and prospector and sometimes of the roughneck." He told the people in Fairbanks that he had no idea that Alaska would be such a good place for families, praising the "incomparable American childhood" and the "matchless American womanhood."

"I presume the explanation for the magnificent specimens of youthful Americans that I see everywhere in Alaska may be found in the open life which is led here, in the inspiration of environment, in the boundlessness of their hopes, and in the wonders of the Alaskan climate, with its long nights in the winter during which they may grow and the long days of the summer during which they may play. There are compensations in all things. God must have worked it out. I have come to the conclusion that you need your long winters," Harding said. At another stop in Fairbanks, Harding inspected the medical facilities at St. Joseph's Hospital. "Mr. President, may I take a picture of the hand that leads the nation?" a doctor asked him. Then the doctor placed the hand that led the nation in front of the x-ray machine and produced a good image of its inner structure.

Harding's wife, known as the "Duchess," didn't participate in any of the Fairbanks ceremonies. It was said she was too weakened from the rail trip to enjoy much excitement. As the train pulled out of Fairbanks, Harding's last words were "Good luck to you." Harding's luck was about to run out. He ate tainted crab meat on a stop at Cordova and the homeopath traveling in his party may have increased the strain on his heart by treating him with purgatives. The scandal-ridden Harding administration ended when he died in San Francisco, sixteen days after leaving Fairbanks. The most serious corruption cases surfaced after Harding's death, as did additional revelations about what his attorney general labeled as numerous "women scrapes."

In Fairbanks, the exhilaration of July turned to grief in August at the death of a man described by the *News-Miner* as the "First President of Alaska."

The realization soon grew that the railroad would not bring immediate prosperity back to Fairbanks, but it did open the way for the town's revival over the next few years. The railroad brought cheaper year-round transportation to Fairbanks and gave access to a reliable supply of coal, reducing the dependence on wood, which was becoming scarce in the immediate area.

The railroad also led to a new era in mining, a more mechanized and large-scale industry far removed from the pick-and-shovel days. Norman Stines, a square-jawed mining engineer, was among those who recognized great potential where others saw a worked-out mining camp of abandoned claims. He didn't resuscitate Fairbanks by himself, but he did more than anyone else to lead the charge. A committee headed by a U.S. Bureau of Mines official estimated in 1919 that although gold production had continued to decline, more than $100 million in gold remained in the ground near Fairbanks in low-grade deposits.

Fairbanks Daily News-Miner

Norman Stines

Conventional wisdom held that areas that had proved profitable for drift mining could later be dredged at a profit, but the lack of water in the semiarid region and the thick overburden made large-scale dredging impossible in Fairbanks. Impossible, that is, until Stines and others began securing support for an elaborate water supply and ditch system that would divert water from the Chatanika River to Fairbanks and bring back the mining industry.

The second generation of miners in Fairbanks knew they had to operate on a large scale to make a profit. They had to start thinking big. At the head of the list of the big operators stood the Boston-based firm known as the United States Smelting Refining and Mining Co., which had holdings in Chicago, Utah, California, New Mexico, Alaska, and elsewhere. Its Alaska operations were conducted by its subsidiary, the Fairbanks Exploration Co., known in Fairbanks as the FE Co.

"It is not fair to say that dredging lacks the romance of other forms of mining: rather, it should be said that dredging is the story of hard-won triumph, framed against a background of precise economic and engineering planning; whereas drift mining and much open cut mining are often opportunism with the element of chance predominating," Charles Herbert wrote in his thoughtful 1934 thesis on gold dredging in Alaska.

The "precise economic and engineering planning" led to the construction of the Davidson Ditch, one of the most ambitious projects of the age. James Davidson, a civil engineer, convinced Stines that large quantities of water could be brought to Fairbanks and that was the key to developing a profitable dredging operation, along with rail transportation.

Joseph Lippincott, a California engineer who helped build the 250-mile-long Los Angeles Aqueduct, designed the Davidson Ditch, a water pipeline and channel system that stretched for ninety miles across hills and valleys north of Fairbanks. When completed in 1928, this engineering marvel carried 875 gallons of water per second to the creeks, enough water to create ponds where massive dredges could float. Inverted siphons allowed water to flow through pipes down one side of a valley and up the other, relying on the same principle that allowed people to siphon gas from a tank with a rubber hose. The siphons transported water from one hillside down into a valley and up over the other side of the valley. There were fifteen inverted siphons, a tunnel seven-tenths of a mile long, and eighty-three miles of ditching, carrying water at a depth of nearly four feet.

Tractors and graders dug through the moss, frozen muck, and rock to carve what was in essence a temporary river. The diesel shovels on the job had seen previous duty in digging the Panama Canal. The final cost climbed to more than $3 million, or about $36,500 per mile, about twice the early estimates. Leonhard Seppala, the great dog musher, used his dog team on early inspection trips of the ditch route. There were frequent breaks in the ditch that had to be repaired quickly to keep the water flowing and the mining operations afloat.

Large-scale mining in Fairbanks required about five years of advance work, an investment of more than $10 million, several dredges, and the massive administrative and legal chore of acquiring thousands of mining claims. Even with the tremendous costs, the company could expect a $21 million profit over the life of the dredges, Stines estimated.

"It was a big ante but the stake was high and it was decided to stay in the game," George Mixter, vice president of United States Smelting Refining and Mining, wrote later.

The Davidson Ditch, an engineering marvel of its time, carried water to the mining grounds north of Fairbanks. This siphon crossed the Chatanika River.

By the mid-1920s, there were predictions that large-scale dredging would bring "20 to 40 years of prosperity" to Fairbanks. As it was, the FE Co. became the dominant factor in the revival of Fairbanks, buying most of the old mining claims on nearby creeks and becoming the town's largest employer. Historian Clark Spence said the dredges "applied the mass production of Henry Ford's America to gold mining," with huge machines processing gravel that couldn't be worked in any other way. It was mining on a scale that would have been unrecognizable to Felix Pedro and other early prospectors. To small operators, the claims were not profitable because there was too much gravel and not enough gold.

It was all in finding the most efficient way of moving gravel, and the FE Co. excelled at this task. In its first six years, the Fairbanks dredges operated ninety percent of the time throughout the mining season, Spence wrote, a better record than most dredging companies throughout the world. He said because of its attention to detail and efficiency, the FE ranked as the "gold dredging operation par excellence in Alaska."

At peak operations, the FE Co. dredges chewed through 75,000 tons of gravel and stripped 175,000 tons of muck per day. No longer was success determined by whether a miner found the richest spots to shovel. The pay streak was not measured in feet, but in acres.

"There was a transition from individual endeavor to cooperative company operation," writer Merle Colby said in 1939. "The colorful, adventuresome prospector is not seen so often; in his stead are high-salaried business executives."

Miriam Dickey, an assistant to the town's leading businessman, Austin E. "Cap" Lathrop, said at first there were feelings of resentment and defiance among many of those who held the old mining claims that had been drift mined in the early years. "They had vague ideas about what this insidious thing CAPITAL would do to the country. But the resentment was short-lived when they were offered attractive sums for claims which had been stripped of their high-grade pay and were worthless to the small miner," she said.

The FE Co. built a large complex just north of Fairbanks, installing the largest power plant in Alaska, which burned 250 tons of coal a day. By 1937 the company had more than fifty miles of power lines carrying power to the dredges on the creeks. The company also built the biggest machine shop in Fairbanks along with mine construction camps and maintenance facilities to keep the huge dredges in operation.

The company compound on the Steese Highway, now Illinois Street, included four houses for its executives, warehouses, a concrete block office building, and other facilities. During its heyday, the company employed about one-third of Fairbanks' population. The FE Co. and its managers changed the town in other ways, too. "They were an asset to the commu-

Gold dredges floated in their own ponds, digging for gold and spewing gravel by the ton. The repeating patterns are still visible decades later along the bottoms of the gold-bearing creeks.

nity," pioneer Jessie Bloom said. "They were not in the least inclined to 'high hat' the pioneers and they added the right kind of incentive to the development of the town esthetically." They became involved in the PTA, the social clubs, the fraternal organizations, and "it took no time until everyone was acting as though they had lived in the town for years."

Dredging began in 1928 at Chatanika, Gilmore, and Goldstream. Additional dredges started digging at Fox and Cleary in 1929. After determining how much gold was in the ground by systematic drilling of test holes, the company begin removing the so-called "overburden," which took from one to three seasons, depending on depth.

Huge nozzles called "giants" washed away millions of tons of dirt, which was flushed into streambeds in the Tanana River drainage. "No serious debris or ecology problems existed because the major rivers of

Interior Alaska have many tributaries which originate from active glaciers and the silt introduced by the stripping operations was relatively small compared to that introduced by the glaciers," Jack Boswell, manager of the Fairbanks operation, contended.

Boswell argued that dredging improved the ecology because at many spots clay was dumped on top of the gravel, providing a place where willows and aspen could take root. The *News-Miner* suggested in 1939 that one day the land scarred by mining might be a long and level expanse in the Ester area, "improved with the greens and hazards of a deluxe golf course or the runways of a transcontinental airport, only 12 miles from Fairbanks."

These old interpretations of the benign influence of dredging aren't accepted by many today who regard large expanses of ugly tailings as eyesores and evidence of environmental destruction of the past. The company and its supporters always emphasized the positive economic aspects of dredging, which kept the community from going broke. "Later generations find it easy to criticize and fail to understand that in earlier years environment was not an issue where gold dredging was concerned," Spence wrote in his history of Alaska dredging.

The water supply to strip the mining ground at Ester, Gold Hill, and Cripple Creek came from the Chena River, where a pumping station was built (now the site of the Chena Pump House Restaurant) to divert the water up to ten miles to Ester. The Chena Pump Station at one point used as much power in a week as the city of Fairbanks used in a month. The dragline assembled at Cripple Creek weighed more than 767 tons and was the largest in North America and the second largest in the world.

There were some complaints in Fairbanks about the silt that was returned to the Chena River by a ditch that emptied below the pump station. "Their contention is that this muck is light and would be carried off with the water," said Henri Dale. He said the "accumulated deposit of muck freezes and becomes hard as granite" in the winter, making spring floods worse. Even he admitted, however, that few people in Fairbanks objected to the practice. The staunchest defenders of the dredges had to admit that the many acres of tailings piles left behind by the dredges, which were piled in windrows of gravel, had a barren appearance, but in most minds the damage to the landscape was an insignificant price to

The huge dredges brought prosperity to Fairbanks for decades, mining low grade gold deposits.

pay for the great economic benefits of mining.

The goal of the elaborate process was to remove the deposits of silt and dirt that had built up over millions of years and to get down to the gravel of the ancient streambeds where the gold was found. At Cripple Creek, the FE crews washed away up to 140 feet of muck. One man at the controls and a helper could run the Cripple dragline, which did the work of a thousand men with No. 2 shovels.

With the overburden and muck removed, the miners drove steel pipes into the frozen gravel that carried cold water into the ground, thawing the gravel over a period of weeks. With the gravel thawed, the dredges, which had been assembled on site from equipment shipped via the railroad, could start operation. The giant boats, which looked like big buildings with long trunks on the front and back, excavated gravel, separated the gold, and deposited the tailings in the rear. On the front of each dredge was a long arm with steel buckets that reached out and cut into the gravel, carrying rocks into the dredge in assembly-line fashion. Standing inside a dredge was like being inside a factory. The noise of all the rocks and the moving machinery was thunderous. The dredges were so efficient that a local joke told of a man being scooped up by the clawing monster and coming out in one piece, but missing his four gold teeth.

Dredges floated in ponds that needed a constant supply of fresh water to keep the mud down; the pond gradually moved along with the dredge as nearly all of the material removed by the buckets in the front was dumped out the back in mounds. The mounds formed a repeating pattern, reforming the valleys into gravel piles, some of which are still visible near Fox and other areas near Fairbanks.

The dredges operated twenty-four hours a day on three shifts from late March to early December. At night in the fall, they were lit like houseboats and could be seen and heard from great distances. Dredge operators had a "religious fervor," one miner said, to keep shutdowns to a minimum because they only made money when they were digging gravel.

The line of buckets in the front could reach up to 70 feet below water on the largest dredge, which chewed up 10,000 cubic yards per day. A typical dredge crew consisted of a dredgemaster, three winchmen, three oilers, four deckhands, a panner, and two shoremen. A visitor to one of the FE camps said the food was almost as good as was found on cruise ships with "veritable rowboats of beef, pork, lamb, potatoes, vegetables—which no doubt come by the ton from Outside—ketchup by the quart, gravies and sauces, arm-straining dishes of stewed fruit, pies, cakes big enough for a golden wedding, and sundry other appetite-quenchers which I have forgotten, passed, mostly in silence, from hand to hand up and down the long table."

Successful operation of a dredge depended on the winchman's skill in maneuvering the dredge to stay in position to get a full load of gravel in the buckets. Charles Herbert wrote, "Just as some pilots appear to handle a plane as well as a bird handles its body, so some winchmen make a dredge appear to be an animated monster. Perhaps the best test of a winchman's ability is a count of the number of empty buckets that come up when he steps ahead."

Herbert compared the dredgemaster to a mine shift boss. He had to be a good mechanic and an expert in handling the dredge, making sure the winchmen kept the boat running at full production and that no valuable bedrock was missed. The panner was responsible for the tables where gold was collected and he had to take samples from the bucket line and pan the gold to determine that the winchman was digging deep enough.

"While most dredgemen have pride in their work and as a class of labor are unusually reliable, it is wise to have automatic recording devices to serve as checks against operation," Herbert wrote.

One of those used in Fairbanks was an automatic depth recorder that showed each step of the dredge. About once every two weeks dredges would shut down for a "cleanup" when trusted workers collected the gold and took it to town in locked steel boxes. Gold shipments went to San Francisco as registered mail at two cents an ounce, a typical gold bar costing about $18 in postage.

The biggest key to the prosperous FE Co. era came in 1933 when President Franklin Roosevelt devalued the dollar and raised the price of gold to $35 an ounce. This insulated Fairbanks from the worst ravages of the Great Depression and created jobs and expanded mining operations at a time when there were bread lines throughout the nation. There was a saying that "Alaska never knew the Depression."

Along with higher gold prices during the FDR years came the end of Prohibition. The NC Co. advertised "What's good with Beer!", an approach that suggested that maybe there were those who didn't know. The company offered the following suggestions: Kraft's Swiss Cheese, Blue Moon Cheese Spread, Salami Sausage, Cheese Wafers, Butter Pretzels, Plain and Stuffed Queen Olives, Bread and Butter Pickles, Imported Sardines, Tegar Chicken, Hormel Ham, and Hormel Pigs Feet.

In Fairbanks, businessmen liked to say that while they had heard of the Depression Outside, Fairbanks took the "De" and the "I" out of Depression, which left them with the words "Press On." When Roosevelt was inaugurated, a bank holiday was declared, but the First National Bank of Fairbanks declared that it didn't need one.

Fairbanks did not entirely escape the economic downturn of the 1930s, as evidenced by the ten percent pay cut the FE Co. instituted in May 1933 that lasted for nearly a year. By 1937, however, the town's largest employer was paying employees about twenty-two percent more than it had in 1929. Nearly 1,000 people had their names on the FE Co. payroll. Dredging reached an all-time peak in 1940, when the big machines produced 209,000 ounces of gold in the Fairbanks area.

The relatively good times in Fairbanks led to an increase in job seekers from Outside and an even greater jump in the number of people inquiring about prospects of getting work. It was not unusual for the Chamber of Commerce to get fifty such letters in one mail delivery. In the last three months of 1938, 500 letters poured in, most of them from people looking for work. A group of men made the trip every spring from Outside to try to escape the Depression, and they would congregate on the Cushman Street Bridge while waiting for work. Bob Redding recalled that the men would carve their initials in the wood and he remembered one who wrote "Money low. Work soon? D.M. 1934."

A visiting congressman was not far from the mark when he said that because the town subsisted on gold mining, "you are one of the few communities in the world that has not suffered from the business depression." The FE Co. was the salvation of Fairbanks, according to the *News-Miner*, which never hesitated to point it out. When Ernest Gruening, a former newspaperman, became governor of Alaska, he visited Fairbanks and was interviewed by a *News-Miner* reporter.

"After I had given him my statement, I asked him about journalism in Fairbanks and asked him what must nots, 'keep outs,' and Sacred Cows there were. He looked at me somewhat in surprise and I recalled to him that I was a newspaperman. He then said, 'Nothing whatever unfavorable to the FE or any of its officials. The same for Northern Commercial, and practically nothing about labor.'" There was also nothing unfavorable about Cap Lathrop, for he had owned the paper since 1929, in addition to the movie theaters, the coal mine, the new radio station, and the new Lathrop Building. Born a year after the Civil War ended, Lathrop had left school at age fifteen and came to Alaska in 1896. He started a theater in Cordova and later added theaters in Anchorage and Fairbanks. He was not usually quoted verbatim because his vocabulary, one of his employees wrote, "had much in common with a roman candle."

After learning about the news situation in Fairbanks, Gruening wrote in his diary that this is a "swell state of affairs" since the FE and the NC companies "practically control the economic life of Fairbanks and the entire surrounding country, plus the fact that they practically dominate the legislative delegation from the Fourth Division." ■

Being a Good Sport

A wide range of sports attracted players and fans from the early days, including tennis, curling, ice skating, and baseball. At First and Wickersham, where the Wickersham Banquet Hall is today, tennis players played on an outdoor wooden court, enclosed with a fence about fifteen feet high on the ends. Ladies played in long white dresses, while men wore white pants and shirts as they darted back and forth on the boards. Another tennis court, with two asphalt-surfaced courts, was built in the 1930s at Fourth Avenue and Cowles Street.

Those interested in the strenuous life in Fairbanks could play indoor baseball in the winter, where stakes might be a couple of boxes of Havana cigars. The annual midnight sun baseball game highlighted the outdoor season from Fairbanks' earliest years. In a 1908 account, players had "the blistering rays of the midnight sun beating down upon them, their every move followed intently by a crowd of wild fans whose enthusiasm held them in the oven-like bleachers." In the winter, there were tournaments for billiards, pool, bottle pool, whist, cribbage, and chess at the Tanana Club, while bowlers aimed for pins at the California Saloon and boxing tournaments. The Tanana Club had boxing, but that was stopped by members who wanted more privacy in the comfy confines of the club on Saturday nights.

The Fairbanks Curling Club, established in 1905, is one of the oldest sporting organizations in Alaska. The sport was played first on the NC Dock between Barnette Street and Turner. Later it was played on the river ice and in 1908 a curling club was built on Second Avenue between Cowles and Wickersham. There was skiing and ski jumping in the 1930s on Birch Hill, with an Anchorage man once jumping nearly seventy-four feet. An organized hockey program started in the 1930s. Teams played on the Chena River, but waiting for the river to freeze and the chore of building the rink and taking it down in the spring led the hockey players to build a rink on donated land on Garden Island. Basketball started in 1908 with several men's and women's teams formed by members of the Arctic Brotherhood, a fraternal organization. In the 1920s, the Alaska Agricultural College and School of Mines established its team, and the chief rivalry on the court for many years was between the College Polar Bears and the town teams. ■

On the Silver Screen

The tombstone read "KELLY" on top and below it, "Goodbye Old Friend, Dick." It was a dramatic gesture that was entirely appropriate given the theatrical manner of the friend who put it there. He was Dick Thorne, Fairbanks' first movie mogul, a man whose calling in life was to entertain others. "Dick Thorne is known to Yukoners and Alaskans as one of the most capable, legitimate actors and showmen who ever came north," his obituary read.

In his early years, Thorne took to the stage in London and South Africa, performing Shakespeare. He joined the Klondike gold rush, setting up in Dawson with organist and conductor Ernest Sarreile.

He was a striking figure, who wore his hair long and when he was shorn of his locks by people who wanted to give him a hard time, he made the most of the publicity. "HAIRCUT GIVEN TO DICK THORNE" read the *News-Miner* headline.

This happened when Thorne reached Iditarod on the steamer *White* and "a bunch of practical jokers, having an expressed antipathy toward an overabundance of hirsute, took charge of him, with the result that the veteran showman is now only an ordinary, everyday personage."

Thorne organized stage shows in Dawson and Fairbanks and later went into the movie business, presenting the latest features in the Orpheum Theater, which could seat 400. Thorne opened one of his establishments July 10, 1915 at Gordon's Rink, showing *Tillie's Punctured Romance*, the first Charlie Chaplin movie to be seen in Fairbanks. Admission was fifty cents to see the man described locally as "the funniest man on the stage today."

Early in the days of silent movies in Fairbanks, Thorne would stand up near the screen and use his pointer and read the captions aloud to make sure that everyone could follow them. In one movie there was a tense scene in which a child heroine died. When one word flashed upon the screen, Thorne put his heart into a painful wail and cried "Dead!"

A man in the audience yelled out, "Is that what it says Dick?"

The crowd began laughing when they should have been crying and

Thorne gave up the practice of pointing and reciting the words to silent movies. From then on, he stuck to the piano music.

When the showman walked about the streets in Fairbanks, he was usually accompanied by a supporting actor named Kelly, a friendly white poodle. When Kelly died, Thorne buried him in his backyard and put a marker over the spot to bid farewell to his old friend.

The man who followed Thorne as the leading movie mogul in Fairbanks was not an actor, but he was the richest man in the territory. In 1927, Cap Lathrop opened the Empress Theatre, the first building in Fairbanks made of reinforced concrete. It was in the Empress Theatre where silent movies flashed along during their final years and where the era of the "talkies" began. The first movie shown in Fairbanks that people didn't have to read captions to understand or have someone stand at the screen with a pointer was the first Marx Brothers film, *The Cocoanuts*, which played in Fairbanks in 1930.

Fairbanks Daily News-Miner

Austin E. "Cap" Lathrop

Hearing sounds with movies created a "tingle that failed to wear off," one viewer said. Theater manager Don Adler said "talkies" were great, but people would have to get used to not talking among themselves during the movies.

"You've got to hand it to the Old Man for what he's done for Fairbanks," Adler said of his boss, Cap Lathrop. "He could have put up a theater that cost one third of what this one did and at that we'd still be having a theater more modern than most towns Outside of twice and three times the population."

A *News-Miner* editor, also referring to his boss, said Lathrop realized that "sound means more to his audiences than it can ever mean to an audience where that which is portrayed is available in actuality." ∎

Alaska Railroad

President Warren G. Harding drove the golden spike commemorating completion of the Alaska Railroad. In his address, he said, "It is not possible to liken a railroad to a magician's wand, but the effect to me is the same, for the whole problem of civilization, the development of resources, and the awakening of communities lies in transportation."

Most Air-Minded City

For more than a quarter of a century, Weeks Field was the home for the aviation industry in what became known as America's "Most Air-Minded City."

In the weeks before the October 1929 stock market crash, volunteers in Fairbanks made an investment in their future that they hoped would pay big dividends. On October 3, the mayor declared an "airworthy holiday" and asked all able-bodied citizens to bring pitchforks, axes, and shovels to a field just south of town near where Lathrop High School and Hunter Elementary School are today. Dozens of residents, including the president of the college and his deans, answered the call.

The volunteers used the holiday to create a Fairbanks landing field for the 775-foot *Graf Zeppelin*, a giant dirigible more than three times as long as a Boeing 747. Before it was permanently grounded after the *Hindenburg* disaster in 1936, the *Graf Zeppelin* made nearly 600 flights, covering more than one million miles at speeds of up to 80 mph. Passengers enjoyed the spacious lounge and dining car aboard the dirigible as well as the red carpet and the windows that slanted in so travelers could watch the ground.

A group called the Aeroarctic Society, which had representatives from 20 nations, wanted to hire the *Graf Zeppelin* for a 16,000-mile flight to foster research by 35 scientists. "From Fairbanks it will fly in a great circle around the polar regions and then return to the terminal point at Fairbanks, where the ship will be refueled and necessary repairs made," a German-language newspaper reported.

It was the hope of making that flight a reality that led Fairbanks citizens to take pitchforks and axes out to the field. Businessman Austin E. "Cap" Lathrop had purchased sixty acres south of town, near Weeks Field, as a landing site. "We cannot fall down on the construction of this field now," Lathrop said. "The Zeppelin flight is the greatest thing ever offered to this city."

The FE Co. donated a bulldozer, driver, and fuel to clear the round track needed to allow the ship to pivot on the ground. It would be held fast at the front, attached to a sixty-foot wooden mast placed in a concrete base. The rear would move with the wind like a weather vane, so the zeppelin would always be facing into the wind.

Eight concrete anchors nine feet by seven feet were poured in late October, making the field ready for the zeppelin. In later years during construction of schools and a swimming pool, contractors bumped into these anchors, unexpected reminders of a forgotten investment.

"As the landing of a Zeppelin is no easy matter," the *News-Miner* advised readers, "a volunteer arrangement will have to be worked out whereby about 200 men will respond when a whistle is blown, signaling the Zeppelin is in sight. Ropes are thrown from the Zep and it is pulled down by the ground crew."

Fairbanksans never heard that whistle blow, and volunteers never got the chance to come running and pull in the *Graf Zeppelin*. After the stock market crash, plans for the trip fell through and Fairbanks was left

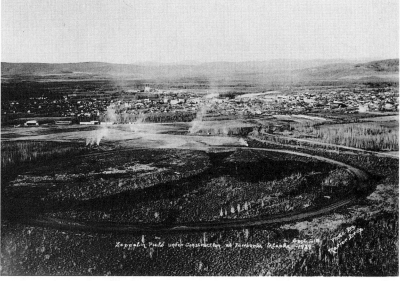

A field south of Fairbanks was transformed into a circular landing track for a dirigible in 1929.

with its landing field. But the enthusiasm over the zeppelin project was in keeping with the optimism that people in Fairbanks had regarding any development related to aviation.

Few people on earth welcomed the age of flight more energetically than the residents of Fairbanks. Traveling by air was so much faster and more convenient than mushing dogs, riding in a horse-drawn sleigh, or pushing a car out of the mud that Fairbanksans were eager converts to air travel. There was only one real road in the territory at the time, the Richardson Highway to Valdez.

In explaining his willing acceptance of aviation, Sam O. White, the first flying wildlife agent, described a typical predicament for an Alaskan traveler. "I came down the Yukon in a canoe one time to Eagle and started walking to Fairbanks," he once told an interviewer about his 200-mile walk. "About halfway there this airplane flew over me and I figured, 'You know, that fellow's gonna be in Fairbanks in about an hour and it'll take me about a week.' That was that. I started taking flying lessons from Noel (Wien) and his brother Ralph and got me a plane." White retired from commercial aviation in 1963, when he was seventy. The new mode of travel that he and others in Fairbanks adopted with eagerness had its first halting appearance in the mining camp in 1913.

That summer three Fairbanks businessmen hired an aviator to ship his biplane from Seattle and perform demonstration flights as the highlight for the town's Fourth of July bash. Many people in Fairbanks had never seen an airplane before and the businessmen who formed the Fairbanks Amusement Co. figured they could recoup the cost of bringing Captain James Martin to town by charging $2.50 for adults and $1 for children under 15 to watch the plane fly. Infants in their mothers' arms would be admitted free.

While in Fairbanks, Martin spoke on the history of the airplane since the Wright Brothers first flew and how he had promoted an aviation meet in Boston at which pilots competed for a $5,000 prize and dropped dummy bombs. Martin warned Fairbanksans to keep a safe distance from his thirty-foot-long airplane. "The speed of my machine is about a mile a minute over the ground so that you will easily recognize how dangerous it would be to have any spectators in the way," he said.

The flights took place at what was then called Exposition Park (later Weeks Field) at 10th and Cowles, used for baseball games, horse races, and marathons. Some of the sourdoughs gathered for the exhibition had doubts about whether flight was real or some kind of trick. Edby Davis, who watched the first flight, said that Martin had trouble getting his plane going at first and someone bellowed out, "It's a fake."

Davis said there were about 250 paying customers and about 2,000 other people who watched for free from the nearby NC Co. wood yard and assorted rooftops as Martin soared for 9 minutes, climbing up to about 400 feet. Davis was among the 2,000 who felt no need to pay. He said there were nearly as many non-paying spectators the next two days, even though admission was cut to $1, leaving the promoters with a financial loss from the first flight. The *News-Miner* bemoaned the lack of paying customers as a "shame and disgrace," especially because most people had never seen an airplane. For the rest of his life, Davis would occasionally think of the man who yelled, "It's a fake" and how wrong he was about flying machines.

In 1910, a writer called upon to envision what Fairbanks would look like in 1930, predicted that it would be the hub of four or five railroads and that local farmers would supply all the town's food. He also predicted the winters would be warmer because of a change in the climate, that Alaska would be a state and the town would have its own airline with daily trips to the coast.

He came closest to being correct with his airline prediction because aviation grew rapidly once it reached a practical stage in the 1920s, thanks to the pioneering work of men like Carl Ben Eielson, who became America's leading Arctic pilot, Noel Wien, Harold Gillam, Joe Crosson, and others.

Eielson was twenty-five when he arrived in Alaska in 1922 to teach science in the Fairbanks High School. He had grown up in North Dakota and enlisted in the air service in World War I to be trained as a pilot. He did some barnstorming after the war and completed college before heading to Fairbanks. His desire to fly drew the attention of two Fairbanks businessmen who wanted to put the town on the aviation map— R.C. Wood, president of the First National Bank, and W.F. Thompson, editor of the *News-Miner*. Wood and Thompson formed the Farthest North Airplane Co., with Eielson as pilot, and they ordered an airplane, a World War I surplus Curtiss Jenny that arrived in June 1923.

A decade after Martin made the first flight in Alaska, Eielson also took to the skies from the park that had been named Weeks Field in honor of Secretary of War John Weeks of Massachusetts. Weeks, described by one historian as a "wealthy Massachusetts broker-turned-politician of respectable mediocrity," declined an invitation from Fairbanks to attend the dedication ceremony, but he did give his permission to have the field named after him.

Weeks was the top federal figure in aviation circles and the Fairbanks aviation boosters figured that it wouldn't hurt to have a friend in high places. They dreamed of buying a fleet of airplanes and starting an aviation school, citing statistics to show that flying was safe and cheaper than driving a car. "Fairbanks today has all the running gear necessary to take its place at the top of the aviation enterprises in the United States," Thompson said. "We have the men who have the price to buy the 'ships' and the willingness to do so."

Fairbanks Daily News-Miner

Carl "Ben" Eielson, who came to Fairbanks as a teacher, recorded many firsts in his brief flying career. With Hubert Wilkins, he made the first flight from Alaska to Spitzbergen, Norway.

102

After the airplane arrived, Eielson made his first flight on July 3, 1923. He flew to Nenana the next day and made it in an hour-and-a-half, slowed by what others would later describe as a poor sense of direction. Eielson flew to mining camps and villages that summer, but the real test occurred the following winter when he flew the first experimental air mail route in Alaska. Eielson believed that the airplane would revolutionize mail delivery in Alaska by making villages that had waited for weeks and months for letters accessible in a day. The government loaned a De Havilland DH-4 biplane for the flights from Fairbanks to McGrath and pledged $2 a pound for delivering the mail.

Eielson wore two pairs of wool socks, a pair of caribou skin socks, moccasins that reached to his knees, a suit of long underwear, khaki breeches, trousers made of Hudson Bay duffel, a heavy shirt, a sweater, a marten skin cap, goggles, and a loose reindeer-skin parka with a wolverine fur hood. He also wore light woolen gloves and heavy fur mitts. With all those clothes on, he was too hot, even with the heater turned off in the open cockpit plane.

He carried 164 pounds of mail for McGrath on the first flight in February, along with emergency supplies that included a sleeping bag, a 10-day supply of food, a gun, an ax, and tools. Eielson made the flight to

UAF Archives / Bunnell Collection

Carl "Ben" Eielson used this De Havilland DH-4 biplane for the first air mail flights in Alaska in February 1924. The government paid Eielson $2 a pound to deliver the mail.

McGrath, following the Tanana River to Nenana and then going cross-country, in about two hours and fifty minutes, covering 315 miles. One of those who saw him out on the trail was Fred Milligan, who had carried the mail by dog team for twenty years. Eielson waved to him from the plane as he flew out of sight. A few hours later Eielson passed him again, this time going the other way. "I decided then and there that Alaska was no country for dogs," said Milligan, who later became an airport traffic manager for Pan American.

On the return flight Eielson lost his bearings and admitted he "wandered around completely lost for almost an hour." He saw a light from a cabin and figured he was near the Chatanika River, so he turned back to find the Tanana River and saw something in the distance. A bonfire lit in front of the hangar helped guide him into Weeks Field, but he guessed where the edge of the field was in the dark and broke a ski on a tree as he glided in. The plane nosed over and the propeller broke, but he was unhurt. In a single day he had covered more distance than a dog team could in weeks, completing the first of what would become a series of eight air mail flights over the next three months. He had a few rough landings on soft snow and mud that banged up the plane. Alaskans judged the flights a success and were ready for regular air mail, but post office inspectors concluded that the service wasn't safe just yet.

Later that year the principals of the Farthest North Airplane Co.—pilot Eielson, banker Wood, and newspaperman Thompson—proposed a bold plan. They believed it would take the "king of stunts" to capture the world's attention, so they proposed a flight to the North Pole and back. Thompson asked Arthur Brisbane, a columnist for the Hearst newspapers, if Hearst would pay $10,000 to finance the trip.

Thompson summarized the 2,000-mile trip this way: "Start Sunday morning in July (after prayers): plant the American flag squarely on the snoot of the North Pole (in the name of the Hearst publications, *Baltimore News* or U.S. Govt.) and be back in Fairbanks the following Saturday in time for the weekly bath; COST $10,000." Thompson said that the North Pole weather was warmer than that in Fairbanks, "almost too warm for comfort for our flier, who has flown here at 40 or worse below in his specially-heated suit and darned near died from the heat."

Nothing came of the flight, which for $10,000 of Hearst money would have been billed as the "Hearst-*Fairbanks News-Miner* Polar flight," but Eielson did become the first pilot to fly across the Arctic Ocean. He earned his greatest fame by completing a 2,500-mile flight from Alaska to Spitzbergen with explorer Hubert Wilkins. In 1928, a year after Charles Lindbergh flew the Atlantic, Eielson received the Distinguished Flying Cross for what was called "one of the most extraordinary accomplishments in all time." Without radio contact or any outside support, they completed a flight that Gen. Henry "Hap" Arnold said was second to none for "sheer nerve and phenomenal daring."

Eielson went on to make the first flights over Antarctica before returning to Alaska and forming an airline in Fairbanks in 1929, the year the zeppelin field was built. He died that fall at the age of thirty-two when he crashed on a flight to an icebound ship off the Russian coast, more than 1,100 miles northwest of Fairbanks. The ship carried a valuable load of furs and Eielson's company planned to make up to fifteen flights to haul them to market. Eielson's body was returned to Fairbanks and he lay in state at the Legion Hall. At the request of his father, American and Soviet flags draped the casket, an acknowledgment of the Soviets' help in retrieving his body.

After Eielson's death, there was a petition to rename Weeks Field as Eielson Field because "The name Weeks Field has no significance and means nothing to the citizens of Fairbanks generally, and an opportunity exists to perpetuate the name of our late beloved citizen, Carl Ben Eielson."

The city council did not go along with the change, but in 1931 it did legally establish Weeks Field as an airport instead of a park. It also bought the NC wood yard for $200 to expand the airfield. Sixteen years later the Veterans of Foreign Wars in Fairbanks petitioned to have a new military airfield, known first as 26-Mile or Satellite Field, named for Eielson. The American Legion Post went along with that suggestion, as did the U.S. government.

The pioneering work of Eielson was followed by that of Noel Wien, a Minnesota farm boy who made the first nonstop flight from Anchorage to Fairbanks in 1924. Wien was a mild-mannered and quiet man whose personality was at odds from the image of the swashbuckling devil-may-care bush pilot. Bob Reeve, who was at the other end of the personality scale and would say "Let's vamoose" to slow-moving passengers, once praised Wien by saying, "I have never heard Noel Wien raise his voice to any man and I've seen him take guff that would make the Pope cuss his mother."

For his first flight to Fairbanks, Wien followed the tracks of the Alaska Railroad much of the way. About three hours out of Anchorage, he ran into heavy smoke and had to fly looking down at the railroad tracks. He knew he was in Fairbanks when he saw the experimental farm near the college and the NC Co. smokestack, completing a flight that took three hours and forty-five minutes.

News-Miner editor Thompson said that one day it would be common to fly between Anchorage and Fairbanks and that the Golden Heart City would be the "aviation center of America." Within a few years, pilots from the aviation center were making flights over Mount McKinley, the tallest peak on the continent. On the second such trip, Joe Crosson flew about 100 feet over the summit, allowing newsreel cameramen to take film of the snow-capped peak in August. The pilot and cameramen had headaches the next day, but otherwise they were fine, recommending oxygen for future flights.

Pilots had to be resourceful and sometimes had to forget what it said in the textbooks. Al Bramstedt Sr., a pioneer broadcaster, once wrote of a trip he took with bush pilot Frank Barr from Fairbanks to Eagle. After unloading the mail, liquor, food, and fuel, Barr taxied to the end of the strip and got eight or nine Eagle residents to hang onto the tail and the skis while he revved the engine. Volunteers held on as long as possible, allowing the plane to start with a jump and get up enough speed to take off from the short strip.

The early pilots also faced a constant struggle that had nothing to do with the weather, equipment breakdowns, or the lack of landing lights on the Fairbanks airport. That was to keep from going broke. As one executive put it in 1931 to a Congressional hearing in Fairbanks, "Flying in Alaska has been a tremendous business failure but a 100 percent success from an operating standpoint." Arthur

Johnson of Alaskan Airways said his company's planes flew 40,000 to 50,000 miles per month in the winter, conclusively proving that "airplanes are cheaper and safer than dog teams."

"We have licked temperature in aviation; we in Alaska can teach the war department and the world the handling of internal combustion engines in cold weather. We do believe air transportation has possibilities in this territory, and we think in time it will become a business success," Johnson said.

Pacific Alaska Airways, the Alaska subsidiary of Pan American, grew to be the largest carrier flying out of Fairbanks. It had five miles of aviation routes for every mile of road in the territory and started air mail service between Juneau and Fairbanks in 1938. In one month, the PAA Electras carried 84,000 air mail letters, the postage on which was twice that of ordinary letters. Pan American Airways envisioned Fairbanks would become an air crossroads of the world, with flights from Europe and Asia making regular stops in the Golden Heart City.

Fairbanks was still a log cabin town of 3,000 people with dirt roads in the late 1930s, but there were more than four dozen airplanes based at Weeks Field and more flying than in many towns of 100,000. It was said that airplanes were to Fairbanks what taxicabs were to New York City.

"In a way Fairbanks is the most important aviation center in the world," Mayor Les Nerland told a reporter in 1940. "Fairbanks people fly more miles per capita than any other people on earth. We are the hub of Alaska flying and we constitute one of the most important aviation crossroads of the Northern Hemisphere. The skies are our most practical highways."

The pilots and passengers traveling those highways in the skies included miners, prospectors, villagers, and also world travelers, who dropped in from time to time. It is only apparent to those who look at the world as a globe, instead of as a two-dimensional map, but Fairbanks is about midway between New York and Tokyo.

World fliers from Wiley Post to Howard Hughes made stops in Fairbanks while circling the globe. In 1933, Post stopped in Fairbanks while flying around the world by himself in the *Winnie Mae*, completing the journey in a little less than eight days.

Five years later, Howard Hughes, who was then a flamboyant 34-

Fairbanks citizens crowded around Howard Hughes' airplane when he stopped during his 1938 round-the-world flight. He took on fuel and unloaded emergency gear.

year-old millionaire and not the reclusive billionaire of later years, set the round-the-world record with a crew of four, circling the globe in a little under four days. He said that his flight was not as significant as Post's solo flight. "What Post did was something like sawing a woman in half or pulling a rabbit out of a hat," said Hughes.

When Hughes stopped in Fairbanks, town leaders spoke with him while bystanders scurried near his Lockheed 14 aircraft to scoop up some of the thousands of ping-pong balls he had carried to provide emergency flotation in case he had to ditch in the ocean. Hughes also dumped sleeping bags, canteens, boxes of food, numerous pieces of luggage, chairs, flares, a box of oranges, a rubber boat, heavy clothing, and other emergency supplies to reduce weight.

As it was, his plane, weighed down with five and a half tons of fuel, barely cleared the trees at the end of the runway on Weeks Field. Some town leaders took the close call as evidence of the airport's deficiencies and they warned that there would be real trouble in the future when "super planes with four motors and 32-passenger capacity" tried to fly to

Fairbanks. The improvements did not come, however, and by 1944 the head of civil aviation in Alaska said that Weeks Field, barely adequate for a DC-3, didn't deserve to be called an airport.

Looking at the Weeks Field neighborhood as it stands today, dominated by the Fairview Manor housing complex, the Noel Wien Library, a park, and the converted and enlarged Pan American hangar that became the Arctic Bowl, there are few signs that it was once the busiest airport in Alaska. It took many years to get federal approval and federal money for a new airport. By the late 1940s, work was underway to build a new airport on top of Chena Ridge, today a prime residential area. Several people filed homesteads just before the land was withdrawn for the airport, which caused a local controversy. The Chena Ridge plan was discarded, however, and the airport was built after the war on flat ground east of Chena Ridge near the Tanana River, far enough from the city to allow for the growth of Fairbanks.

If Alaska's place in world geography was crucial to the bold pilots who competed to set aviation records, it was also much on the minds of those who knew that if aviation could serve the interests of peace, it could also serve the interests of war.

Brig. Gen. William "Billy" Mitchell learned about Alaska when he worked on the early telegraph lines that connected military posts in the territory in 1902-03. He went on to serve with the U.S. Army Air Service in World War I and became a tireless proponent of air power. By lashing out at Army generals who stifled aviation and Navy admirals who objected to his claim that "sea power was done for," Mitchell created enough enemies to get court-martialed, but he continued to make his case without mincing words.

"It does not take much of a look into the future to see that he who holds Alaska holds the world, because a great expanding nation, if it becomes dominant in the air, can now achieve world domination more easily than the United States established in its present confines," Mitchell said.

Mitchell promoted the successful 1920 flight of four military biplanes from New York to Nome and back, by way of Fairbanks. The flight established the first air link to Alaska, followed by the first world flight in 1924, which skirted the Alaska coast, and by a 1934 flight of B-

10 bombers from Washington, D.C. to Fairbanks.

One goal of the 1934 mission of the blue-and-yellow bombers, under the command of Lt. Col. Henry "Hap" Arnold, was to scout for potential airfield sites. Arnold, who later was commanding general of the Army Air Forces during World War II, wrote that he was visited by a stranger in Fairbanks while waiting for the rain to stop.

The stranger, a German immigrant who had drifted around the world, was a pilot in Fairbanks. He had inspected the all-metal 200-mph Martin bombers flown by Arnold and his men and found them lacking. "What would you say if I told you the Germans have a far better bomber today than you have in that B-10 out there?" the man asked.

"I couldn't say anything, except you're a damn liar," Arnold replied.

The Fairbanks pilot insisted and urged Arnold to ask American officials in Germany to visit the Junkers plant, the Heinkle plant, or the Dornier Plant and inspect what the German government was calling "high altitude transport planes." The Fairbanks man only smiled when Mitchell said that allied inspectors had been checking German factories to make sure that war planes were not being produced.

Arnold wrote in his autobiography that this conversation "took my breath away." After returning to Washington, Arnold informed U.S. intelligence of what the Fairbanks pilot had told him. The next spring the Nazis announced that the German Air Force was to be recreated, and they promised that it would be the strongest in the world.

After the trip Arnold recommended that an air base be built in Fairbanks, to support the air defense of Alaska and for cold-weather testing. Additional bases should be built in Anchorage and Juneau, he said. A small but growing number of politicians and military leaders had begun to believe that Billy Mitchell, who died in 1935, may have been right when he said that Alaska was the most strategic place in the world. Congress, however, did not see war clouds in Europe as reason to act with urgency. ■

FAIRBANKS, ALASKA.   Will Rogers Leonard Seppala   Wiley Post   Joe Crosson

Fairbanks Daily News-Miner

Will Rogers, left, and Wiley Post, second from right, before their takeoff on the Chena River, a flight that ended in their deaths. Talking with them are dog musher Leonhard Seppala, second form left, and Joe Crosson, right.

Farewell to Will Rogers

The plane landed on the Chena River outside of Fairbanks and one of the most popular men in America stepped out of the red single-engine craft and looked around with a grin. "Is that all the river you got?" Will Rogers said. "Gotta have more river than that for an airplane."

Although the fifty-five-year-old Rogers was one of the biggest names in Hollywood, he looked right at home as he ambled the streets of Fairbanks, giving away silver dollars to the crowd of children who followed him everywhere. He wore plain clothes and looked a little like a miner in from the hills, taking in the sights of the city. Rogers and Wiley Post, one of the greatest aviators of the time, stopped in Fairbanks in August 1935 while on their way to Siberia. Post had been in the city twice before on his daring round-the-world flights in 1931 and 1933. Rogers was not only the biggest male movie star of the early 1930s, he was also a popular radio commentator, newspaper columnist, and an expert at cowboy rope tricks. During his life he wrote more than 2 million words for publication. He often started his columns with the sentence, "Well, all I know is just what I read in the papers."

He wrote many variations of this, including one he typed in Alaska: "Well, all I know is just what I hear when I talk to somebody and as I generally do all the talking, why I don't hear much, but I started out on this trip with the idea that I was going to do some listening." Rogers wrote his last daily and weekly newspaper columns in Fairbanks. He praised Fairbanks as the "greatest aviation-minded city of its size in the world" and wrote about flying with Wiley's friend Joe Crosson, who had come to Post's aid on his previous flights. Rogers took a flightseeing trip with Crosson past Mount McKinley and visited the Matanuska farm colonists, discovering "there is a lot of difference in pioneering for gold and pioneering for spinach."

Rogers spent a lot of time walking around Fairbanks and told people that Post and he were just "bumming around." He donated $100 to the Fairbanks baseball team and stopped by the elevator in the federal building, just to ride it up and down. The operator, Virginia Rochester, stayed with the Crossons and worked in the kitchen to help with the rent. Rogers was mashing potatoes for her when she told him about how proud she was of her elevator and asked if he would stop by for a ride. Rogers said he really liked Fairbanks and the Chamber of Commerce "didn't annoy me at all while I was here." Post and Rogers took off from the Chena and flew to Harding Lake, where there was more room to take off with a full load of fuel. They flew north and landed about fifteen miles from Barrow to ask for directions. Post took off again, but the engine sputtered and the float plane crashed into the ground, killing both men.

The last column Rogers was writing was in his typewriter, unfinished at the time of the wreck. It was a story about meeting dog musher Leonhard Seppala, who "is as identified with dogs as Mae West is with buxomness." He closed with comments about dog mushing and the story of a dog named Mickey who belonged to the Crossons and who got tangled up with a bear and ran home, so "the first thing you know you got a bear in your lap and a dog between your feet." The unfinished column, found in his typewriter in the wreckage, stopped at the word "death." ■

9

Through Dust and Mud

Second Avenue was unpaved in 1938, and Fairbanks residents voted to keep it that way.

The powder kicked up by the 1,000 cars and trucks on the streets of Fairbanks in 1937 was such that pilots said they could sometimes see clouds of dust eighty miles out from the Fairbanks airport. Voters went to the polls in Fairbanks that year to decide whether to start paving streets and pull the town out of the mud. The city planned the first pavement for stretches of Second Avenue and Cushman Street.

The federal government offered an $18,000 grant and the city intended to raise an additional $27,000 by selling bonds that would be paid off by the property owners bordering the streets to be paved.

"There is too much grass growing on the streets of Fairbanks, so let's pave them," said Lipman Simpson. Another resident agreed and said Fairbanks should become "an up to date town and not a shacktown" and fix the streets. But opponents like Gordon Springbett said paved streets were "absolutely unnecessary at this time."

Fairbanks voters, with a well-deserved reputation for being contrarians, approved an addition to the school, sewer improvements, and the replacement of more wooden sidewalks in that 1937 election, but they concluded that Fairbanks wasn't ready for paved streets. The vote was 134-126 to stick with dirt. Mayor E.B. Collins, angered at the prospect of more mud, said that in previous years he received many phone calls about why the streets were such a mess. Those days were over. "I want to hear no complaints from now on about the streets being filled with water and in an impassable condition when it rains," the mayor said.

After another year of downtown mud and dust, however, the city again tried the paving proposition and succeeded. In 1938, Fairbanks accepted the prestige of pavement. The measure passed 120-43 and by the summer of 1940, Fairbanks drivers could roll over more than a quarter-mile of modern pavement. Though Fairbanks hailed the new road surface as "the most costly stride toward being a real city," it was almost insignificant compared to another paving project a few miles away. A drastic change, as far-reaching as the original gold rush and the rebirth brought by the railroad, was taking shape in a clearing in the woods to the southeast. After years of indecision, the government had decided it needed to build new military facilities in Alaska. A modern runway was nearing completion outside of Fairbanks, one of the first steps in establishing a cold weather test station to be known as Ladd Field.

Almost as soon as the Army announced the name of the new field, chosen to honor an Army pilot named Arthur Ladd who died in South Carolina in 1935 and had never been near Alaska, the Fairbanks Chamber of Commerce asked that it be changed to McClellan Field, in honor of Capt. Hez McClellan, who died in a crash in Ohio. He had flown Army planes to Alaska in 1934 and 1935 and did some of the early scout-

Ice Carnival Throne at night
Fairbanks, Alaska - 1939

In 1939, Fairbanks organized an annual Winter Carnival. Preparations included an elaborate ice throne honoring pioneers chosen as King and Queen Regent.

ing for the Fairbanks base. People thought it would be easy to simply switch the names of the Alaska field with the California field to be named after McClellan, but the military was unmoved by that logic.

Years of prodding Congress led to the decision in 1937 to reserve six square miles between the Richardson Highway and the Chena River for the Army, including all or part of the Spencer, Buzby, Badger, Junes, and Dittman homesteads. The Richardson Highway had been re-routed to go around the new field. Fairbanks was selected as a site for the station because it was in a broad valley, had little fog and good flying weather, and it was cold in the winter, a prerequisite for a cold weather test station. The idea was to train pilots and mechanics to maintain and operate planes in cold weather. When approval finally came, it turned into a rush order. Surveys began in 1939, and workers finished the runway by the fall of 1940. Work had continued through the winter and the Fairbanks mayor credited the Army personnel with an achievement that was "nothing short of amazing."

In the summer, more than 1,000 men worked in three shifts. The nation wasn't at war yet, but the growing conflicts overseas created a sense of urgency about the lack of preparedness.

Maj. Dale Gaffney, base commander and the man for whom Gaffney Road is named, landed the first plane on the Ladd runway on Sept. 5, 1940. "The largest slab in the territory of Alaska," as the *News-Miner* called it, was inaugurated when Gaffney touched down in a O-38 observation plane.

The work in Alaska was long overdue, according to Alaska Delegate Anthony Dimond, who said spending money to build up defense facilities at Pearl Harbor but not Alaska was akin to locking one door of a house and leaving the other open. In the fall of 1938, the *News-Miner* voiced worries that Japan's aggression in the Pacific and its alliance with Germany and Italy would leave Alaska more vulnerable than Hawaii or the Panama Canal.

The next year the threat seemed closer than ever. Nine days after Hitler invaded Poland in September 1939, starting the war in Europe, speakers at an American Legion banquet in Fairbanks called for caution.

Fairbanks Daily News-Miner

The Alaska Railroad Depot, located where the Fairbanks Daily News-Miner is today, was a vital center for the comings and goings of the town and its main line to the "Outside."

Don Adler, the Alaska commander of the American Legion, said that all those who had fought in World War I prayed that their sons would not have to go through the same horrors.

"Overseas there is another World War going on. We may be in it in a few months; we may never get into it. I know it is the desire of every ex-service man to keep America out of the war," he said. "We, who have tasted of death on the lines, we don't want to see American boys taste of those same experiences. We must guard our children lest they pick up the expression 'Germans are no good.' We have Germans and other citizens of foreign birth in this town who are just as substantial Americans as the best of us American born."

He said that no one should criticize an entire nation because of the actions of a "worthless few."

With Hitler trying to conquer Europe, Maj. Gen. Henry "Hap" Arnold returned to Fairbanks in 1940 to check on progress at Ladd Field. "I sincerely hope that this vast scheme of national air defense in which Alaska is destined to play a vital part will never be needed in the defense of our country," Arnold said in Fairbanks. "If we have an adequate defense in the air, there is less likelihood that we will be attacked. Air defense is national insurance. The recent wars have taught us one lesson which our people should never forget. That is, that the flying machine, one of the finest vessels of air commerce, can be turned into the deadliest weapon of war."

The work on the Ladd runway and the assorted buildings on the field developed into the largest, most costly, and most complicated construction project in Fairbanks up to that time. The officers on the ground had orders to build the base as quickly as possible. The original base buildings were laid out like a horseshoe, with the hangar at the open end of the horseshoe, and the shop, power plant, warehouse, and barracks buildings close by. The utilities were underground in a tunnel, directly beneath the sidewalks. The underground passageways had multiple uses. "The beauty of the whole plan, and the original idea, is there was no snow to shovel because any heat loss in the utilidor would melt the snow and kept the sidewalks safe for walking," said Randy Acord, a Ladd field test pilot.

117

Arnold said the engineers quickly learned how to work in cold weather and the base would be a great help to the air corps once the men had the right gear. "We believe, from reports of our observers who have watched fighting in the Arctic climes, that special clothing must be devised. There are fewer than 250 suits of the proper type of clothing obtainable in all Alaska," he said.

Despite the positive public comments about how well the project proceeded, there were also bitter complaints to the governor and Congress from Fairbanks workers about how the job had been run and allegations of excessive waste and unfair treatment of Alaskans. "If all the defense projects in the United States are conducted as unfairly and inefficiently as that at Ladd Field, Mexico could come up here and whip us with one arm tied behind her," a Ladd construction worker said.

S.K. Harrod, who fought in World War I and was wounded in France, served in the Army until 1929 when he went into private business. He was the foreman in charge of the dirt-moving machinery at Ladd before he was laid off. He said he was treated unfairly, but he insisted that he wasn't just an unhappy ex-employee. He wrote to Delegate Anthony Dimond and Governor Ernest Gruening with allegations of costly engineering and management mistakes. "I know that over and over again one shift would put in its time doing something which would be undone by the following shift and then perhaps changed still again on the third shift, due to the lack of competent and intelligent supervision of the 'engineers.'"

He said two expensive paving machines were purchased, but only one was ever needed. The other one sat out in the weather from spring until summer and "was still there the last time I saw it, rusting away in idleness." He also said that the people doing the hiring showed favoritism to workers imported from the Outside. "I know that there has been on these projects a deep-seated prejudice against all Alaskans, no matter how competent, and that this prejudice has cost the government scores of thousands of dollars. These projects, far from helping the rank and file of Alaskans, as should have been the case, have been very detrimental to their well-being, due to the asinine method in which the employment situation was handled," Harrod said in a letter sent in December 1940. He claimed that hundreds of men, some with their wives and children, were shipped up at government expense and that when layoffs took place, the Alaskans were the first to go. Another worker claimed that more than half of the Ladd field workers were not from Alaska. He said Fairbanks businessmen didn't demand that Alaskans be hired and "were afraid to take any concerted action lest they antagonize the men in charge."

Harrod added that in Fairbanks, a town "where there is certainly no prudish concern over such a little thing as hard-drinking," certain of the Ladd field construction bosses were well-known for excessive use of alcohol. Joe Flakne, director of the territorial employment service, reviewed the complaints for the governor. "His statements agree with what other workmen have said, it seems that Mr. Harrod is correct," Flakne wrote.

Similar complaints about excessive spending, waste, unfair hiring practices, and "cost plus fixed fee" contracts were raised about the many military and civil aviation construction projects underway at the time throughout Alaska. In 1940, however, it was easy to get a job in Fairbanks. Old-timer W.E. Geiger said it had never been like that in the entire history of the town or at Nome or Dawson during the gold rushes: "At no place in Alaska, except in this city, at no time except for now, could a man want-

Candy Waugaman Collection

On the shortest day of the year, the sun creeps above the southern horizon. Local photographers take multiple images tracking the sun's path during the three-hour-and-forty-five minute day.

ing a job walk right into it for a season. Fairbanks now is the best camp Alaska has ever known."

In April 1941, *Newsweek* ran a photograph with a caption stating there were 4,000 troops in Fairbanks. The *Anchorage Times* corrected this by reporting that the main military installation was in Anchorage and there was a "small camp" in Fairbanks.

"Ladd Field officers admit that 'something less' than 300 troops are stationed here," Fairbanksan G.N. Meyers said, "but they do not agree with the *Times'* designation of the United States Army Air Corps Cold Weather Experiment Station as a 'small camp.' And neither do I."

Military began to appear in large numbers in Fairbanks for the first time. "You saw them downtown in olive drab uniform, soldiers on a Saturday night spree," Bob Redding recalled. "You met their motor caravans along the highways, you saw their aircraft overhead."

At that time the most popular magazines for sale out of the 350 offered at the Red Cross Drug Store were *Life* and *Reader's Digest*.

"What interests folks for the most part is what can be instantly visualized or briefly stated," said proprietor Frank Dunham. "Are we mentally indolent? No, just busy." ∎

10

War on the Home Front

In the 1940s, the University of Alaska campus was still fairly remote from the bustle of downtown Fairbanks. KFAR's transmitter tower was just to the north of the campus.

The first person in Fairbanks to learn of the Japanese attack on Pearl Harbor was Augie Hiebert, an engineer on duty at radio station KFAR on the morning of December 7, 1941. Hiebert and another young engineer lived at the KFAR transmitter on Farmers Loop, which looked out on a rolling valley of snow-covered spruce trees where Cap Lathrop planned to put a golf course some day.

Hiebert was tuning the dials on a short-wave receiver and listening to a radio drama that morning when an announcer interrupted with news of a real-life drama that shocked the world. Hiebert ran to the next room to tell Chief Engineer Stan Bennett about the radio reports that Japanese planes had bombed Pearl Harbor. "They must be crazy," Bennett said, immediately starting to scan frequencies for confirmation.

He found it by listening to short-wave Morse code news messages flashed from New York by TransRadio Press, which supplied radio news for Fairbanks. Until midnight that day, Hiebert and Bennett kept busy taking down the news reports in dots and dashes at forty to forty-five words per minute about the attack on Hawaii.

The radio engineers called Army authorities at Ladd Field, who in turn called the Alaska Defense Command in Anchorage. By early afternoon Col. Dale Gaffney, Ladd Field commander, arrived at the station with guards and began issuing written orders for broadcast as Fairbanks prepared for a possible attack. "There was every expectation that key communication points, such as KFAR's transmitter site, would be taken by paratroopers. We had no idea that they weren't going to capture Alaska," Bennett said.

Gaffney ordered people to use phones only for emergencies, to stay off the streets as much as possible, and to immediately report any sign of subversive activities. He dispatched soldiers to guard the power plant, the radio station, the federal building, and the telegraph office. Volunteer guards soon replaced troops because Gaffney said he had "three jobs for every man" at the base.

"Fear was upon us," one resident said, "not a personal fear but a definite foreboding of bad days ahead for Alaska."

Fairbanks was nearing the shortest days of the year, when the sun barely peeped above the horizon in the south and set within four hours. The hostess of the regular KFAR woman's hour radio program the next day started by saying that when disaster threatens, people shed "all smallnesses like shabby old coats."

She went on to express the emotions that many people felt: "Those of us who have lived here for some years have seen great changes. The

John Kowalak

The wartime boom brought increased traffic to Second Avenue in downtown Fairbanks.

work at the base has provided employment for many and brought added prosperity to the town. To some it has given the means of buying things really needed; to others it has meant having more than a few luxuries. We've all screamed about the inefficiencies and needless waste in this same defense work, but now it has given us a measure of protection," she said. "We have enjoyed referring to ourselves as Uncle Sam's stepchildren. Maybe we are, but the old boy's arms are around us now and even a stepfather's arms, when they happen to be Uncle Sam's, can feel very good."

On the day the U.S. declared war on Japan, more than 200 men signed up for civil defense work in Fairbanks. Led by Lou Joy, amateur radio operators in outlying areas served as an early warning system to be on the lookout for enemy aircraft. Forbes Baker, head of the American Legion Emergency Squadron, arranged volunteer guards to replace the soldiers at key city installations. A separate civil defense squad formed across the river in Graehl under the leadership of Ted Lambert. For the next month up to sixty men stood guard duty at night.

Barricades blocked the airport runway whenever a plane was not landing or taking off. This was to prevent enemy planes from capturing the field. Gaffney also ordered barricades placed at Creamer's Dairy, Bentley Dairy, the University of Alaska, the experimental farm, and on all straight stretches of the Richardson Highway up to eight miles from Fairbanks.

Dozens of men and women volunteered to join the Red Cross. The audience at the Empress Theater on December 8, 1941 cheered a week-old newsreel that talked about the U.S. Navy as the greatest in the world.

Neon lights and outdoor display lights were banned and a city blackout was called for December 10. Power usage dropped fifty percent during the blackout, leading civil defense officials to announce that people had missed the point. They were supposed to keep their lights on inside their houses and to make sure that no light could be seen from the outside. Blackout wardens policed the effort, but within seconds after the NC alarm sounded, ninety percent of the city went dark.

Bud Foster and Al Bramstedt stationed themselves on the roof of the Lathrop Building with microphones, looking for wayward lights. Residents used dark blankets, black paper, and wood to cover their windows and they stopped stirring fires in their stoves because any sparks could be seen by the enemy. "The next blackout may or may not be practice and 100 percent effectiveness will be necessary," the *News-Miner* reported.

Ten days after Pearl Harbor, Civil Defense headquarters gave the OK for businesses to have neon lights for Christmas, as long as they went off at midnight. After Christmas, blackouts became a nightly feature. With snow on the ground, however, even the darkest night was never completely blacked out as the snow always reflected a little light.

The NC steam siren, used for years as a fire alarm, served as the air raid and blackout warning signal. Citizens filled bags with sand and kept a shovel, a pail of water, goggles, leather gloves, and a ladder on hand in case bombs started fires. Jeff Studdert had a large supply of sand in his basement to give away to those who needed more.

"Fairbanks has been a shining mark, visible for hundreds of miles to any flier approaching the city at night," the *News-Miner* said. "This must be no more, and not even a candle glowing where it can be seen."

Civil defense officials told drivers to learn how to disconnect the distributor cap and tear out ignition wiring in their cars before an attack. During blackouts motorists covered their headlights to make them dim blue. At the University of Alaska, the faculty members of the civil engineering department offered to help the Army and a home guard unit started to watch the campus. With the temperature close to fifty below, President Charles Bunnell warned that "Under the present circumstances there is more danger of freezing to death than getting shot."

During that dark December, some in Fairbanks took comfort in the words of the poem *Invictus* by William Henley:

"Out of the night that covers me,
Black as the Pit from pole to pole,
I thank whatever gods may be,
For my unconquerable soul."

The city council held a special meeting on New Year's Eve to adopt blackout rules, the violation of which carried a fine of $100, thirty days in jail, or both. The talk of having gas masks led some people to look on the bright side; gas masks could double as dust masks in the summer.

The war effort generated such strong community support that a few days later, the city held an election at which the vote was 88-1 to make a gift to the federal government of land along the Chena River, just upstream from the Cushman Street Bridge, for a USO.

Throughout January, people made emergency plans to evacuate the town in case of attack and head for the hills. Then came the orders that wives and children of military men and of civilian construction workers at Ladd Field had to go to the States. In the months that followed, some of the wives drifted back to take military jobs, some of them using maiden names to sidestep the red tape.

The war changed Fairbanks permanently and for many residents it became a great dividing line of social and economic change.

Between 1941 and 1945, the United States spent $1 billion on Alaskan defenses. We learned later that the Japanese had no plans to invade the continent through Alaska, but the U.S. did not know that at the time. The bombing of Dutch Harbor, 650 miles southwest of Kodiak, six months after the Pearl Harbor attack, brought the war close to home. The Japanese effort in the Aleutians was both an attempt to draw American naval forces north in a diversion and a way of preventing use of the Aleutians as a base to bomb Japan.

The Army centered Alaska's defenses at Fort Richardson and Elmendorf Field on the outskirts of Anchorage, but facilities in many parts of the Territory figured into the overall war plan. In the face of worries that Alaska might become a "second Pearl Harbor," the long-dreamed-of Alaska Highway became a reality in nine months. It followed an inland route that would connect air fields used to supply the "Alaska Skyway," the aerial path to Alaska.

Visiting Fairbanks less than three weeks after the war started, George Sundborg, a senior planning technician for the Natural Resources Planning Board, found a community where the economy had been controlled by three interests and now the military made four. "This situation is a result of the old trader system carried to an extreme and perfected by modern methods. Three interests—the FE (Fairbanks Exploration division of the U.S. Smelting, Refining and Mining Company), the NC (Northern Commercial Company, which owns the utilities and the largest store) and Cap Lathrop—have Fairbanks in a stranglehold," Sundborg said. "They control the newspaper, the radio station, the banks, the Chamber of Commerce, the merchants, the life and breath of Fairbanks.

"What is to be done about it, I don't know. But there exists a repression which I could actually feel," he told his superiors. He said the merchants "appear to have an agreement that there is only one uniform 'right' price for everything."

Sundborg also said there was dissatisfaction in Fairbanks with the Army for its habit of "coming to town and requisitioning food, supplies or equipment with which it has neglected to provide itself." Sundborg didn't know it, but one of the three dominant forces, the FE Co., was later to become a war-time casualty. In late 1942 the government closed down most gold mining operations in the country, declaring them nonessential to the war effort.

The military leased space in the FE office building and requisitioned draglines, drills, Caterpillar tractors, and other equipment. Fairbanks, which had once been entirely dependent on mining, was now to become largely dependent on military spending. The military wanted Alaskans at Ladd Field because local men knew how to deal with the weather and many of them could handle everything from typewriters to bulldozers, said Robert Redding, who joined the Army in late 1942.

"Going to town was a strange experience for home boys," Redding wrote of his time at Ladd. "For a couple of weeks we had lived in a world entirely different than the one at home. We were regimented in every aspect of our lives from eating to dressing to working, and subject to discipline if we screwed up. Suddenly, we were at home, in our living rooms, having a piece of mom's apple pie, catching up on gossip of the town. The war was far away."

Then when the pass to town was up, they'd be back at the base. "Gradually we learned to synchronize our dual lives, and with tongue in cheek, termed our dilemma, 'The Battle of Ladd Field,'" he said.

Paul Solka, another Fairbanks recruit, said the military didn't insist on perfect specimens of manhood if you had skills in demand. When an examiner, a private first class, asked Solka to read the smallest line he could see on the eye chart, Solka replied, "I can't read any of them."

"Squint," he was told. He did and thought he could make out an "H." The examiner wrote "20/300" on the chart and told Solka that he had passed. So did the thirteen others examined that day. He reported to duty with an empty suitcase and, after two-and-a-half days of basic training, Solka, who had considerable experience in the newspaper business, earned an assignment to the photographic section.

When Redding, Solka, and the others left Ladd to go home, they returned to a town where the hotels were overflowing, the bar business was brisk, and the boom was in full swing by any measure.

There were voluntary "meatless Wednesdays" to conserve the meat supply, and there was also a noticeable increase in crime. "There was a time, not in the too distant past, when it was our proudest boast that locks were not needed, and not used on our doors; that our women and children could go anywhere in town at any time, day or night, unmolested, sure of courteous treatment anywhere, anytime," Ernie Jessen complained in his weekly newspaper. The war boom brought changed circumstances and people began carrying keys. "Locks became such a necessity and so much in demand that we experienced a shortage," Jessen wrote.

There were other shortages born of the boom as well. In 1943, ice dealer Murray Smith ran out of ice, misjudging the need for the cold stuff for the first time in thirty-eight years. "Late in the fall, before the ice on the river was in condition to be 'harvested,' drinkatoriums and other establishments and residents without refrigerating facilities went iceless for a few weeks," a reporter found. "Mr. Smith hadn't foreseen the influx of workers on defense jobs bringing an unusual increase in Fairbanks' population. Result, Fairbanks' first ice famine."

The next winter Smith increased his harvest by twenty percent to 600 tons, which was kept in insulated buildings and used as needed during the summer, being sold for three-quarters of a cent per pound. The supply of ice was within the control of the local ice man because there was never a shortage in the winter. Shortages of other items were more unpredictable. "Some items were tough to get, as far as supplies that you were used to getting, like butter and bacon," Fairbanksan Jim Doogan said. "But we didn't suffer too bad."

It wasn't a matter of suffering, but few people willingly accepted the government decision to censor mail during the war. Letters often arrived with lines blanked out and newspapers reached Fairbanks with stories cut out of them. The absurdity of censoring published reports was that Alaskans could listen to short-wave radio broadcasts from the States containing the same news.

This heavy-handed practice enraged Alaska leaders who discovered there was no statutory authority for censorship between the States and Alaska. The Army controlled Alaska, and sometimes individual rights became expendable. This was shown most clearly in the forced evacuation of the Aleuts and all Alaskans who were at least one-half Japanese. ■

The Wild Blue Yonder

The astronauts who went to the moon in Apollo 15 brought along a faded piece of sheet music from a tune that's as well-known to most Americans as the "Star Spangled Banner."

It was a tribute to Bob Crawford, a boy who grew up in Fairbanks and wrote the U.S. Air Force anthem. The composer's father, a real estate man, joined the Klondike Gold Rush in 1898 and later followed the crowds of gold seekers to Fairbanks with his wife and three-year-old son Bob.

The boy began his music career at seven with a rendition of In the Good Old Summertime. He delivered the *News-Miner* to earn money for violin and piano lessons and later wrote "My Northland," which was adopted by prospectors as a territorial anthem.

Crawford studied music at the Boston Conservatory of Music, Princeton, Juilliard, and in Paris. He wrote serious and light music, performed in Carnegie Hall, conducted symphony orchestras, produced musical comedies, and worked in radio.

A day after learning that *Liberty Magazine* had announced a contest in 1939 to choose an anthem for the Army Air Corps, an idea for a song began to take shape in his mind. He polished it over the next few days and titled it, "What Do You Think of the Air Corps Now?"

It began, "Off we go, into the wild blue yonder, climbing high into the sun. Here they come, zooming to meet our thunder. At 'em boys, give 'er the gun." Crawford's song won the contest and became an immediate hit after he first sang it at the Cleveland Air Races in 1939.

When the Air Force became a separate branch of the service in 1947, the title became "The U.S. Air Force." ∎

The Famous Flock to Fairbanks

A long list of prominent entertainers, politicians, and business leaders visited Fairbanks during the war: Bob Hope, Joe E. Brown, Ingrid Bergman, Eddie Rickenbacker, Lillian Hellman, Dashiell Hammett, Joe Louis, and Vice President Henry Wallace. At one point, President Roosevelt considered meeting Soviet Premier Stalin and English Prime Minister Churchill in Fairbanks, but they decided to rendezvous instead in Yalta.

Louis, the heavyweight boxing champion, recalled how cold he was while touring Alaska and northern Canada in May and June 1945. "If I ever thought Detroit or Chicago were cold, I take it back," said Louis, who gave a $1 tip to a waitress at the Model Cafe and watched a movie at the Lacey Street Theater.

Wallace was the first vice president to visit Fairbanks. His father had toured the city two decades earlier while serving as Secretary of Agriculture under President Warren Harding. The vice president toured the university and Creamer's Dairy. Wallace had

John Kowalak

Boxing champion Joe Louis tests winter foot gear during his 1945 visit. With him is boxer and referee Rudy Goldstein.

brought along volleyballs and a net so that he could exercise. "After dinner, Mr. Wallace issued, on behalf of an American team, a challenge at volleyball with a Russian team," said Stacy Dobrzensky, commanding officer of the 123rd Army Airways Communications System squadron. The U.S. team lost three straight games to the Russians. "We were skunked by a superb team," Dobrzensky said. "During the game, however, the vice president showed a distinct tendency to hog the shots....To our dismay Wallace roved all over the court with 'I got it.'" ∎

Until the Cows Come Home

With the military buildup of World War II came a critical labor shortage in Fairbanks.

Charlie Creamer, who had ninety head of cattle at his modern dairy farm off College Road, couldn't find workers to milk his cows. "Now another very serious situation has arrived, the Army is drafting all the young men," Creamer wrote the governor on Dec. 18, 1941.

The Territorial Employment Service had been looking for a milkman for two months and couldn't find one. Creamer wired Seattle and Olympia employment agencies, but heard nothing back. He was desperate because a man on one of his milk delivery trucks had just received his draft questionnaire. "I am supplying Ladd Field and most of the city. We are running 90 head of stock and we have a large investment, too large to run without help," Creamer wrote. "I have had to take one of the trucks myself and I should be on the place, to

Candy Waugaman Collection

Creamers Dairy supplied the local market and military bases during World War II and beyond. The dairy closed in the 1960s, unable to compete with imported milk. Today the former dairy is a popular wildlife refuge on College Road.

oversee things. It's so hard now at my age to work like this. I will be obliged to cut down the herd of cattle unless there is some way I can keep these men I have trained.

"I had to take my son out of college in March to take one of the delivery trucks. I hated to take him from his school but I could not get anyone, so he had to take a truck. And he had worked every day and Sundays too, all summer," Creamer added.

The governor wrote to Gaffney about the plight of the biggest Fairbanks dairy operation. Gov. Ernest Gruening suggested that women be hired for the dairy farm, but his employment chief told him that the women were all working too. Gaffney replied he was sure "some solution can be worked out so that Creamer will not have to slaughter his cows."

"In view of the fact that he is on the draft board it would appear that the solution would be to defer people that he already has," Gaffney wrote to Gruening.

Creamer managed to keep his farm going through the war and for more than twenty years thereafter, supplying milk and ice cream to Fairbanks, but age and growing competition from milk imported from Outside led to the shutdown of the farm in February 1966.

For many years Creamer had put grain out for migrating birds in his fields and many children grew up in Fairbanks watching the birds. To save the property as a refuge, Fairbanksans raised $7,000 in 1967 to hold an option on 246 acres of property until federal and state funds became available to buy it. The old dairy buildings is now part of the popular Creamer's Field Migratory Waterfowl Refuge. ■

The Key for Alaska's Riches

It looked something like a forest of flagpoles. The skinny poles erected outside many houses did not hold flags, however, but radio antennas that allowed people to sit in their snow-covered cabins and hear the far-off sounds of San Francisco, the BBC from London, and stations from Australia and Japan.

On October 1, 1939, there was another choice on the radio, which was closer to home than the short-wave broadcasts. Cap Lathrop said getting KFAR on the air was the "happiest day of my life." Four months later, Lathrop was almost as happy when he presided at the opening of his Lacey Street Theater only a short walk away on Second Avenue. "Let her roll," Lathrop told the projectionist. Like the movies in the Lacey Street and Empress theaters and the *Daily News-Miner*, Lathrop's KFAR became a central part of life in Fairbanks. Finally there was a station that could be heard on the new car radios in Fairbanks that had only picked up static before. A slogan "Key For Alaska's Riches" had been chosen in a contest and soon the most popular program was *Tundra Topics*, a nightly feature in which personal messages were passed along to people spread over thousands of square miles with no other communications.

The first manager of KFAR was Jack Winston, a former band leader who called himself the "Gentleman from the South" in that former life. His assistant was Bud Foster, age twenty-five, who had achieved a reputation for himself as a master at recreating baseball games in Juneau. In 1939, Foster broadcast the World Series between the New York Yankees and the Cincinnati Reds starting at 9:15 a.m. three days after the station went on the air. There were no live broadcasts in those days, only the brief radio telegraph reports describing who did what in each inning. Foster would take those and spin a tale of high baseball drama that he could see in his mind's eye. He used a studio ball-and-bat device, records of college songs and a recording of cheering to round out the picture.

"When the World Series is on, business almost folds up everywhere in Fairbanks, and as you walk down the street Bud's voice is heard barking over the radios of nearly all the stores in town," writer Jean Potter said. Before KFAR the only radio in the Interior was short-wave, which faded in and out and was unreliable. "There'd be weeks at a time when you couldn't get any radio reception," said engineer Stan Bennett.

A week after KFAR began broadcasting, local stores had sold out of radios, and dealer John Stump said Fairbanks had already become "radio conscious to a remarkable degree." ∎

John Kowalak

Augie Hiebert's dog Sparky barked at the right time to make his presence known on KFAR

11

Red Star Over Fairbanks

Fairbanks Daily News-Miner

The completion of the pioneer road known as the Alaska Highway in 1942 gave Fairbanks a road connection with Canada and a new link to the outside world.

The war drained students and faculty from the University of Alaska for the duration. University enrollment dwindled from a prewar high of 310 in 1940 to less than 70 in 1943.

In 1944, there were not enough volunteers to field a basketball

135

team and there were only three graduates in 1944 and 1945. The School of Mines closed, mirroring the shutdown of the gold mining industry. President Charles Bunnell struggled to keep the university open, compressing its operations into the Eielson Building. Bunnell said the major contributions of the university to the war were "reckoned in terms of men and women who have attended this institution and have answered the call."

About two-thirds of the campus was taken over by the military to help relieve the shortage of facilities on Ladd Field. There was one notable addition to the university course offerings during the war. The school hired a graduate of a Soviet university to teach Russian, a field of study every bit as practical then as mining was a decade earlier. Overnight Fairbanks became a central hub in a major air operation designed to help the Soviet Union fight Hitler. Hundreds of Russian pilots and mechanics, most of whom could not speak English, began flying in and out of Fairbanks on a regular basis.

In June 1941, the Germans launched a surprise attack on the Russians, dealing a crippling blow to the Soviet military. In the months that followed, the Russians pleaded with Washington for help under the "Lend-Lease" program through which American industrial power supplied U.S. allies with billions of dollars of war materials. There was great distrust in the United States of the Soviet Union and antipathy toward Communism, attitudes that were apparent in Fairbanks, but Germany became a far greater threat.

By the fall of 1942, U.S. and Soviet leaders had worked out the details on a plan to use Fairbanks as a transfer point for Lend-Lease aircraft. The peaceful, though sometimes testy, Russian invasion of Fairbanks began. Before it was over, 7,924 planes passed through Fairbanks on their way to the front. The P-40, P-39, and P-63 fighters, A-20 and B-25 bombers, and C-47 transports filled the skies above Fairbanks as they made a roundabout journey to the Eastern Front. American pilots brought the planes to Fairbanks, where the Russians took over.

Nothing about the Russian invasion appeared in Alaska newspapers for a year and it wasn't mentioned on the radio. But there was nothing secret about the planes with the Red Star that constantly flew over Fairbanks on their way to Nome. At one point, according to historian and intelligence officer Otis Hays Jr., a temporary Russian insignia was made

Fighters at Ladd Field await transfer to the Russians as part of the Lend-Lease effort to aid the Soviet Union in its fight against German invaders in World War II.

with the big Texaco star, an emblem borrowed from a service station. Three hundred to five hundred Russian pilots, mechanics, and administrative personnel plus more than 1,000 American technicians handled much of the transfer work in Fairbanks. Base unit quarters built to house 250 troops soon overflowed with 950 men crammed in.

The runway and parking areas at Ladd Field were crowded with planes being put through inspections and final test flights, as the crews from two nations hurried to keep up with the transfer of thousands of planes each year. It was said there were days when the aircraft given to the Soviets were worth more than the original purchase price of Alaska seven decades earlier. The military needed an auxiliary landing field when Ladd Field was closed in by winter ice fog. At a site first called "Satellite" or "Mile 26," and now known as Eielson Air Force Base, crews built additional runways and a hangar to help handle the traffic.

Most of the Russian pilots had combat experience and welcomed

137

ferrying airplanes as a break from battle. One American instructor pilot said the foreign flyers caught on quickly and told how a Russian fighter pilot took off after asking four questions through an interpreter. He wanted to know how to start it, the maximum pressure and RPM for takeoff, how to keep the oil and coolant temperature up, and how to work the radio. He figured the rest out himself.

One of the early Russian arrivals was interpreter Lt. Elena Makarova, who was shocked that American soldiers at Ladd Field whistled at her and another female interpreter. "In the Soviet Union, men whistled at girls whom they considered to be not quite decent, to say the least," she said. "There were so many things to be learned about American customs. We later found out that when American men whistled at you, they did not mean dishonor. We also discovered that all the Americans who knew us had a high opinion of us," Makarova said.

Henry Varnum Poor, a soldier and artist who wrote a book about serving in Alaska during the war, said Russian officers and enlisted men looked different and not only because they wore different uniforms. "Their faces were ruddy like those of American boys, but minus the ease and softness that a life of peace and security and abundant food has given to our boys. This heightened tension, which made their different types seem more pronounced, was, I found, the one ever-present point of difference between us." The mess hall ran round-the-clock due to the irregular schedule. Russians sat at tables to the left and Americans on the right. "Very seldom did any Russian, even one with a little English at his command, sit with the Americans," Poor said.

From outside came the constant sound of motors undergoing tests, with planes landing and taking off at all hours. Poor said the Russian pilots who arrived from the Soviet Union in transport planes, often didn't stay long in Fairbanks, sometimes leaving within a few hours. American pilots, who had infrequent contact with the Soviets, regarded the Russians "as being somewhat arrogant and cavalier about their flying ability, even to the point of being reckless," said Hays.

The Russians demanded that planes be handed over in perfect mechanical condition and would reject them for almost any reason. This created endless bickering at Ladd Field, where the Soviets earned a reputation for being nit-picky about minor problems. According to some, the Russian attitude grew from the knowledge that if anything went wrong with a plane, the Soviet mechanic would be held personally responsible and punished.

"Although the disciplined enlisted men lived under fear of punishment for carelessness or misbehavior, they endured what amounted to Alaskan exile without any sign of being tempted to desert," said Hays. More than 100 Russian pilots died along the 3,500-mile route between Fairbanks and Krasnoyarsk. Hays said that the Soviets regarded time as a "precious element," but he didn't know if their hurry caused the loss of the seventy-three planes. Sixty-eight planes were lost from Montana to Fairbanks, flown by American pilots. One of the first runways on the Russian side was made of wooden planks with gravel between them and the airfield offices were tents pitched off to the side. The flights to Alaska by the American pilots and the flights from Alaska through Russia covered some of the world's most remote territory. In the decades that followed, old wreckage was periodically discovered in the wilderness in Canada, Alaska, and Russia. In one such instance, the remains of a Russian crew and the A-20 bomber they had been flying were found in a remote part of the taiga in Russia in 1987, 3,000 miles from Fairbanks.

Maj. Gen. John Deane, the visiting commander of the U.S. Military Mission to Moscow, said that the Russians controlled about half of Ladd Field. They could go anywhere except where the American planes were parked. Despite the detailed inspections, sometimes there were mechanical breakdowns. Hays wrote of one such incident that made for high drama on the runway. A B-25 bomber captained by Peter Gamov had to turn back in the late summer of 1943 because the nose wheel was dangling.

Hays wrote that the Russian had heard a story about how an American had landed with a similar problem, aided by two trucks on the ground that stretched a rope over the tail of the plane and raced alongside the plane to hold the end down when the plane stopped and prevent damage to the nose of the plane. He called to the Ladd tower, where his future wife, interpreter Elena Makarova, was present, and arranged to have trucks on the runway to try this risky maneuver. "Two trucks were speeding in place when Gamov landed, but his bomber ran freely for half the length of the runway before the trucks caught up and snared the tail with rope," Hays wrote. "Slowly the plane and truck brakes were applied in time to bring the bomber to a halt at the edge of the river."

Though their presence was an official secret, the Soviet pilots became famous in Fairbanks for buying items they hoped to get into the hands of their relatives or friends, without regard for price. They used American cash to buy candy, perfume, soap, cigarettes, women's shoes, canned goods, lingerie, and other items from local stores. One U.S. officer said he was present at a shoe store when a top Soviet colonel asked for shoes. The clerk asked, "What kind?" And the Russian said, "All kinds." The clerk asked "What size?" And the officer replied, "All sizes," leaving his aide to complete the purchase and get it boxed up and taken to Ladd Field. The clerk sold him all of the old lines of shoes that had piled up in the store's inventory.

When not buying in bulk, the Soviets tended to keep to themselves, as there were rules against fraternization with Americans and they were under orders not to go out with American women. The Soviets watched the Americans play baseball and played soccer among themselves. The Soviet officers did use the officers' mess and officers' club, where they enjoyed pool and slot machines. Fairbanks businessman Jim Doogan expressed what was a common sentiment about the Soviet officers in Fairbanks: "They somehow got the idea, many of them, that they were the king of the world and they treated the civilians in Fairbanks about like that."

Gen. Hap Arnold, commanding general of the Army Air Forces, and one of the chief proponents of establishing Ladd Field, had a similar view. "At Fairbanks, Alaska, we leaned over backwards to help the Russians," he said after the war. "We gave them everything it was possible to give them, even turning over to them the houses of our own officers and enlisted men and their families."

He said Soviet leaders never thanked the Americans. "They never showed in any way that they were grateful for what we had done to make their stay in Fairbanks happy and pleasant, or regretted the inconvenience to our people. After the war was over, we practically had to dynamite them out so that we could get our own station back."

Translator David Chavchavadze, a descendant of Catherine the Great who was called up to the U.S. Army after attending Yale, spent a lot of time with the Soviet enlisted men and found them a lonely bunch. He said the translators were always in demand at the movies to explain the lines of comics like Bob Hope. Chavchavadze, then nineteen, and the other translators were part of the "I and I" Detachment, for Interpreters and Interrogators, which they called the "Ay-yay-yay" Detachment.

"We ate together in the mess, but otherwise there was almost no social life. The Soviet enlisted men never went to town," Chavchavadze said. "They must have been lonely and bored. Every night for almost two years there came from the enlisted barracks the sound of an accordion always mournfully playing the same Russian tune, *Siniy Platochek*. This song always reminds me of Fairbanks and the iron curtain already present there."

Chavchavadze, who later worked as a CIA agent for twenty-five years, said the Soviets never gave signs of dissatisfaction with Stalin or his regime. On one occasion, Chavchavadze translated during a meet-

UAF Archives / Byrd Collection

During World War II, Russians stationed in Fairbanks took to the slopes on Birch Hill.

141

ing between Col. Peter Kiselev, one of the Soviet leaders in Fairbanks, and Cap Lathrop.

It was a cordial meeting and both men seemed to respect each other. "On the way back to the base Kiselev was absolutely amazed at Lathrop's control of all the media in town and that these outlets were not plugging any particular line," Chavchavadze said. "The colonel said, nostalgically, that he would like to retire to Fairbanks, build a house for himself, and maybe open a rival radio station."

One of the worst crises during the three-year exercise brought a heavy dose of international intrigue and suspicion to Fairbanks. In July 1943, a Fairbanks taxi driver turned private named John White who had been assigned to the motor pool, drove two Russian intelligence officers past the university to Ballaine Lake. The two officers, a captain and a lieutenant, said they joked with White about his waistline, but didn't communicate much because he didn't speak Russian. The Russians later claimed that they went off to pick flowers and shoot at trees with a small caliber rifle and that when they returned, their driver had disappeared. His clothes were later found alongside the lake and there was a heap of burned cryptographic papers nearby in the trees.

The death of John White would remain a mystery. Searchers found his body eleven days after he disappeared when four million gallons of water had been pumped from Ballaine Lake. White, who had a great fear of water and couldn't swim, had taken off his clothes and gone wading in the lake and drowned. That was the story the Russians put forward, and it was the official explanation given for White's death. A lot of people never believed it. FBI agents in Fairbanks argued that the case required more investigation, but the bureau's Washington headquarters sent this message: "John White Victim. Bureau desires no action be taken this case" and it was signed "Hoover."

There were many theories about what happened to White, ranging from a personal feud to allegations that the Russians had in fact been snooping on communication lines that ran from the university campus to the KFAR transmitter, and they didn't want any witnesses. No charges were ever filed against the two Russians, and they both stayed on the job in Fairbanks after White's death.

Another controversy regarding Lend-Lease arose in 1949 when Maj.

Gen. George Jordan, a liaison officer at Great Falls, charged that some of the planes flown through Fairbanks carried atomic materials and secret documents to the Russians. A congressional committee found no substance to the accusations of espionage, but did report that small amounts of uranium had been shipped with U.S. approval.

Today, there is scant evidence in Fairbanks of the World War II Russian connection that put the town on the supply line to the Soviet Union.

The late Joe Fejes, who worked as an interpreter at the Ladd control tower, said there was one reminder that he could always see in the distance at the Birch Hill Cemetery. It was a large spruce tree that was planted in 1943, a memorial to mark the grave of a tiny child. The tree has long since grown over the tombstone, so that anyone who wants to see it has to crawl through the branches. Her name is Ludmila Yatzkevich.

Some top Soviet officers moved their wives and children to Fairbanks during the war, but the shortage of housing held down the number. Maj. Alexander Yatzkevich, an engineer, was glad to have his wife and their two children, ages three and seven, join him after a long journey. The three-year-old was exhausted and no one recognized the signs of diphtheria until it was too late. She died two weeks after getting to Alaska in 1943. A small coffin was ordered and she was buried on Birch Hill, next to what is now, by Fairbanks standards, a giant tree. The child was one of the millions who can rightly be counted among the victims of World War II.

In August 1945, when Japan surrendered, there was such relief in Fairbanks that peace had come at last, that the town went on a spontaneous spree. The City Council balked at limiting liquor outlets' hours, as had been done for Victory in Europe Day the preceding May. For V-E Day, saloons closed at 2 p.m. and remained shut for twenty-four hours. After Japan was defeated, there was no need to fear complacency. "As long as they don't destroy property, they can celebrate all they want to," said City Councilman Kenneth Murray.

GIs exchanged hats and ties with civilians, officers forgot rank, some businesses put up signs that said "Closed for Victory," and World War I veterans clasped hands with young soldiers. On Fifth Avenue, MPs knocked down the MP sign at their post and "rushed about, howling their exultation," an observer said.

John Kowalak

High-ranking Russian visitors met University of Alaska President Charles Bunnell, second from left, and U.S. military officers on the university campus in 1944.

Chavchavadze, the interpreter, took three Soviet officers downtown to take part in the festivities. "On the main street pandemonium reigned," he said. "GIs, happy and plastered, were wandering around the middle of the street, sitting on car hoods and on the sidewalk, wearing civilian hats and ties. Alcoholic sweetness and light was in the air.

"The Soviets stayed in their Jeep, watching in horror as a group of ten GIs stopped an American captain and with the best good will in the world proceeded to strip him of every bit of brass on his uniform from cap to buttons, slapping him on the back and acting in a very revolutionary manner. The captain adapted quickly, accepting swigs from the soldiers' bottles." The interpreter tried to explain, but he said there was no way the Soviets could understand "this unusual bit of Americana."

For years the Model Cafe had been running around the clock, but it had to close for a few hours after the celebration, to get the place cleaned up for the post-war era. ■

The Long Journey of Francis Harper

Few people ever gave as much thought to the streets and the people of Fairbanks as 1st Lt. Francis Harper. A student at the University of Alaska, he enlisted in the Army after Pearl Harbor and flew 18 missions as a bombardier over Germany. On his last mission he was shot down over Bremen and captured by the Germans.

There were eighteen UA alumni who died in uniform during the war and many others served around the globe. Harper was one of the few who became a prisoner of war. The Germans interrogated him in the middle of the night with a bright light shining in his eyes. It was like a scene out of a war movie, he said.

Harper, born in 1918 in Rampart, was an Alaska Native and one of ten children from a family that is still very much a part of life in Alaska. His uncle, Walter Harper, was the first man to reach the summit of Mount McKinley, a feat he accomplished in 1913. In 1935, his sister, Flora Jane Harper, became the first Native graduate of the Alaska Agricultural College and School of Mines.

Francis Harper wasn't tortured by the Germans, but he suffered during his captivity, losing thirty-eight pounds in eighteen months. He was very weak by the time of his release, as were his friends. "It was painful to see the boys in the showers," he said in 1945, "their legs and arms were just pipe stems."

He received fifty-three letters from home during his imprisonment, nearly all of them heavily censored. Harper took part in at least three unsuccessful escape attempts, one of which started with a tunnel from under a latrine. The men carried the dirt out in small amounts and tried to hide it in the exercise yard.

He occupied his mind by studying, playing an old trumpet another POW had brought from Italy, and reconstructing Fairbanks in his mind. This helped him keep his sanity when he was in solitary confinement, weakened because he was only given bread and water. "I sat in that cell and kept thinking of Fairbanks to keep from going crazy. I visualized the whole city with utmost concentration. Then I mentally walked down Wendell Avenue to Lacey, trying to remember how each house looked and who lived in each one. Thinking of Fairbanks really pulled me through."

He gained his freedom in May 1945 and was shocked to discover that one of his rescuers was a friend he used to play hockey with back in Fairbanks. Forbes Baker Jr. was with the unit that liberated the camp, and he told one of the POWs that he was from Alaska. The POW said he knew of a prisoner from Alaska. Before any names were mentioned, Baker asked, "Francis Harper?"

The old hockey players had an emotional reunion seven hours after the GIs opened the camp. By then, Harper and the other emaciated men were sick from eating the good food they had just been given. "For two hours we just sat around and talked," Baker said. "He was sick most of the time, but he was real happy too. It was a real good reunion."

When he got back to Fairbanks, Harper said he wanted to chop wood, go fishing, and be by himself to get his mind back to normal. One of his sisters recalled hearing him wake up screaming in terror because of a nightmare after the war, but in time his life got back to normal, and he later became the chief accountant with the Bureau of Indian Affairs.

The man who kept his sanity by thinking of the houses and people of Fairbanks died of a heart attack in 1972. ■

12

The End of the Line

HOUSES OF PROSTITUTION, FAIRBANKS, ALASKA, JUNE, 1909

National Archives and Records Administration

"The Line," a Fairbanks institution, traced its origins to the very beginnings of the town. Most citizens accepted the presence of a restricted district for prostitution.

In 1938 the Junior Chamber of Commerce announced a drive for a community center because Fairbanks needed better recreational facilities. The group envisioned a $175,000 center with a swimming pool, artificial ice for skating, auditorium, and space for bowling, basketball, handball, a weight room, and other features.

The ideal location to build this project was the property between Fourth and Fifth Avenues off Cushman Street. "This valuable property is not occupied with existing thriving business enterprises, but covered with unsightly shacks and unoccupied buildings, which have practically no revenue value to the city from taxes," junior chamber members stated.

The rec center proposal did not come to fruition, but the idea of redeveloping the neighborhood to the west of Cushman Street would surface repeatedly in the years that followed. Included in this neighborhood was the Fourth Avenue Line, which had been the restricted district for prostitution almost since the founding of Fairbanks.

At first the talk was of "slum clearance," but later the term of choice for the same thing was "urban renewal." Slum clearance or urban renewal, it dealt with a gold rush relic and many other old cabins built during Fairbanks' younger years. The Line had started within a few years of the founding of Fairbanks as a means of keeping prostitution under control. It survived for a half-century because people argued that prostitution would exist whether or not it was regulated and that it ought to be controlled in some fashion for the public good. A 1906 grand jury report gave an indication of community sentiment: "We strongly protest against licensed women being permitted to live wherever they choose within the city limits and ask that they be immediately restricted to a particular district."

Three years later, a federal immigration official reported that Fairbanks had 3,000 to 4,000 people, 6 churches, 25 saloons, and about 150 prostitutes. He said most of the prostitutes were foreigners and they paid $12.50 a month in a "regular so-called fine, outside of which it is locally reported that other contributions were levied upon them by the police for protection purposes." One of the first times it was pronounced closed was Oct. 8, 1914, when a contractor began tearing down the board fence that separated the cabins from the rest of the town.

"With the abolishment of the 'row' from Fourth Avenue and the tearing down of the fences, there passes from local history a human interest story about which columns could be written. In the world's second greatest gold camp, where close to $70 million in dust has been taken since the year 1903, Fourth Avenue has played no small part. The millions of money that have been

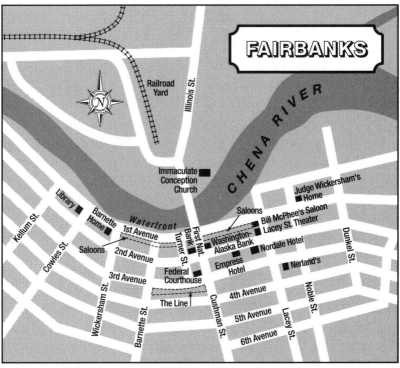

R. L. Walker

"The Line" occupied an area near the downtown commercial district of early Fairbanks.

poured into and out of this short, fenced-in street, with a row of small cabins on each side including two or three famous dance halls, would build a city," the *News-Miner* said. "It has witnessed scenes of thrilling interest, events that would make a drama second to none, fortunes made and lost in a night, adventures and characters beside which the ordinary fiction of the day would read like the *Congressional Record*."

The Fourth Avenue Line, the reporter added, would always have a place in the "profane" history of the North, "never to be forgotten by the sourdoughs who followed the stampede from Dawson here and saw the gold dust lavished with princely hands in the golden days."

But reports of the death of the Line were greatly exaggerated and it remained an institution of note. As late as the 1940s rules approved by Fairbanks city police regulated the life of the prostitutes in the district and required them to register and provide blood tests every three months. To go on vacation they had to report their dates of departure and return to the police chief. They had to stay out of the bars, keep the rear cabin light on every night, and not get drunk during "working hours" from 9 p.m. to 6 a.m. The 1945 rules also required prostitutes to show up at the police station during the first ten days of every month to be charged with vagrancy and pay a $50 fine.

Demands to do away with the Line grew through the 1940s, however, as more people became dissatisfied with the existence of the restricted district. The postwar boom brought the problem to the forefront, especially when the Ladd Field commander warned that the town might be put off-limits to military personnel.

"I think it would be a blow to Fairbanks to be declared off-limits," Ladd commander Gen. Dale Gaffney said at a town forum in 1948, a fantastic understatement. People noticed this threat because it would have meant the loss of the buying power represented by a $1 million monthly payroll. Gaffney, known as the "Screaming Eagle of the Yukon" during the war, had shown he was serious by scheduling maneuvers and alerts that kept personnel away from town on paydays.

Gaffney said more than half of his men were under twenty-one and he would not accept prostitution, wide-open gambling, or liquor violations. He said prostitution had prospered in Fairbanks because of the system of payoffs and that it was time for a new era. Tourism promoter Chuck West asked, "What is to prevent us from running a bulldozer over the whole block?" Not everyone agreed, however, with calling out the bulldozers. Forty years after the gold rush, many people still thought prostitution should be tolerated in a town with thousands of unattached men. They believed it would be best to keep it somewhat under government control.

In a 1947 crackdown, authorities rounded up twenty-three prostitutes and charged them with operating bawdy houses. One of the jurors in the first case, Everett Patton, said years later that there were always "do gooders" who wanted to shut down the Line and they were responsible for the formal charges. According to Patton, the defense attorney gave a powerful closing argument, which included a reference to the Good Book and Jesus' statement that he who was without sin should cast the first stone. The tears were streaming down his face as he spoke. Patton said the lawyer was secretly aided in his work because he had half an onion in each coat pocket and kept rubbing his eyes with onion juice.

In the end not a single conviction resulted from the twenty-three cases, in part because witnesses weren't willing to admit personal knowledge of the Line. This had been a problem every time an anti-Line campaign was launched. "The complaining witnesses would refuse to show up," Mayor Ray Kohler said.

When the police chief was called to testify in the first of the twenty-three cases, he said that "the defendant never discussed her occupation when she paid her fine for disorderly conduct."

The presence of so many single men was cited as a rationale for continuing the Line by some of the town's citizens. "Women who served on the juries told me their daughters would not be safe if the Line were to be closed," prosecutor Harry Arend said. He believed that gambling, liquor, and prostitution were responsible for ninety percent of the town's crime and the problem was growing as the community expanded. The city covered about a square mile, but the areas to the north and south were being settled, though annexation was stymied for many years. Fifteen liquor stores, bars, and nightclubs had sprung up south of town and were all going strong, without much in the way of regulations.

The rapid growth created severe disruptions that would take years to settle out. One petition called for a crackdown on vice; another insisted the status quo was fine. "Along with the military population that has moved into our community there are approximately 5,000 construction workers, builders, boomers and bums which are also Fairbanks' problem," City Councilman R.M. Fenton said.

The deadlock continued for the next four years as more bars and houses of ill-repute set up outside the city limits, away from the Line. A New York-based group called the American Society Hygiene Association began conducting undercover investigations and found that by January 1952, fifteen prostitutes were back in business on the Line.

"Prostitutes were seen in the windows of their crib-like quarters soliciting all potential customers who chanced to pass by," the association said in a complaint to Gov. Ernest Gruening. "Servicemen and construction workers were observed to constitute the bulk of the trade of these resorts." The charges were $10 to $15 except on paydays, when the rates were $20 to $25. "According to many servicemen who were questioned, the line as the prostitution district in Fairbanks is called, was off-limits to military personnel at the time of our study in January 1952. Servicemen stated, however, that the off limits restrictions were not effective and that even if servicemen were denied admission while in uniform they could easily rent civilian clothes from certain cabdrivers."

By then Gen. Donald Smith commanded Ladd Air Force Base, and he again warned the city to take action or else. This time the

The face of Fairbanks has changed a great deal since the 1940s. At the right is the steeple of Immaculate Conception Church, one of the town's landmarks.

city responded more forcefully and within a few months the city manager said that most prostitutes found that it was "too hot" to stay in business and military inspectors confirmed that Fairbanks was losing some of its vices.

The slum clearance project began shortly thereafter as part of Alaska's first urban renewal project. It did not go smoothly, however. For more than five years there were political and court battles over property values and whether the federal government, which was paying most of the bills, had offered a fair price. Ultimately the land between Third and Seventh Avenues was cleared of 130 old cabins. Rebuilding was slow work. By the summer of 1960 it was a "dreary, empty wasteland of leveled-off tracts," one observer said.

The first development on what some had hoped would be a "small-scale Rockefeller Center of the North" was a modern Safeway store, with a seventy-car parking lot and "magic carpet doors which open automatically when entering or leaving the store." The store, which later became the post office and the Laborers Hall, was followed by various projects including a Woolworth's, now the phone company offices, city buildings, a parking lot, and a large J.C. Penneys store. The Penneys store, which featured the first escalator in Fairbanks, remained open for thirty years. ■

John Kowalak

Native women watch Winter Carnival fun from the Cushman Street Bridge.

Winter Wonderland

Fairbanks has often been labeled a land of extremes, which is appropriate, given the weather. The summers proceed at breakneck pace, bringing temperatures that may range into the high nineties, while the winters last for six months and usually bring at least one spell of fifty-below cold.

The prospect of surviving temperatures that are cold enough to turn a cup of coffee tossed into the air to ice crystals before it hits the ground and leave automobile tires frozen flat on the bottom strike fear in many hearts. But there have long been at least two points of view about the Fairbanks weather. One holds that people put up with the horrible winters because the summers are heavenly. The others says that summers are fine, but they live for winter's chill. Writing in 1924, Mary Lee Davis said that she preferred life in Fairbanks in the winter over the summer and that hundreds of others shared this attitude. She quoted a friend who had come from Finland and remarked about Fairbanks, "Summer has been so long. Doesn't it seem as if winter wouldn't ever come? "We who live here the year round come to know and to love our land best in winter, when the quiet fields of space brood in a white unbroken glory, made mauve and blue and rose by phantom day and incredible lights by flickering Aurora in the more lingering dark. Then life is unperturbed by a multiplicity of things that fret our summers; tourists for instance," Davis said.

A decade later, Kay Hufman and Clara West originated the Fairbanks Winter Carnival, a cold weather celebration that became a March tradition. The first carnival lasted three days, highlighted by dog mushing, hockey, dances, and the crowning of a King and Queen regent to preside over the affair. In 1940, Arctic Explorer Vilhjalmur Stefansson set up a vote among students of the winter-happy town about which season they liked the best. The elementary boys and girls showed a strong preference for winter. The high school girls voted 32-23 for the cold season, while the high school boys voted 34-21 for summer.

"It appeared in the wide discussion which followed the vote that parents were divided much as the children, and that the women average a higher preference for winter than the men," Stefansson said. He said he was told the girls liked skating, skiing, and snowshoeing more than the boys. "This was said to have some relation to the particularly attractive and comfortable sports costumes. And here you have one of the main keys to the situation; one does not like any place unless he is comfortable in it; the children of Fairbanks, well dressed for the cold, were more comfortable in January than in July, for you cannot protect yourself similarly from heat. But the July of Fairbanks is the kind of July that many of us like and all of us are used to, which should mean a good deal when we evaluate their testimony on the comparative likability of the different seasons."

There might be a similar split today, although skiing, skating, and dog mushing are popular with both sexes. As temperatures decline through November and December into January, the air is usually so still that you can look over the valley at thousands of trees adorned with snowflakes the way they are adorned with leaves in summer.

Over the years attitudes about how best to cope with winter weather may have varied somewhat. In 1916, for instance, the high school boys debated the

UAF Archives / Metcalf Collection

The snow on the ground didn't prevent Fairbanks residents from taking to the streets in costumes to parade for the "first Annual Railroad Celebration" early in the century.

girls about whether Fairbanks schools needed to teach physical education. The boys took the negative side, saying that all students were already getting good exercise from walking to and from school and doing chores at home. "This side also pointed to the fact that formerly, when the High School had a gymnasium, it was found impractical, owing to the fact that it was too cold with the windows open, and, with them closed, the students perspired to such an extent that when they went outdoors they caught cold," an observer said.

Taking the affirmative , the girls said that if the people of Fairbanks could afford to bet $20,000 on the outcome of the 1916 presidential election, won by Woodrow Wilson, then they could afford a new gym.

Winter is your friend, W.F. Thompson editorialized in the *Daily News-Miner.* "Winter comes every year to remove the germs which form in summer; it has always come and it always will come. Warmth breeds and propagates ill health and winter comes to the rescue in due time and wipes out or minimizes the danger," Thompson said.

The cold is not so bad as it sounds, Georgia Johnson wrote in 1916. "Everyone has his warm fur coat and high arctics, leggings if necessary, and fur cap, so it is impossible to become very cold. Our houses are built mostly of logs and are very warm. Most of them have three or four rooms, which are heated by ordinary stoves, furnaces, or by steam." ■

13

A Town Transformed

Old cabins and modern concrete buildings reflected a contrast in Fairbanks of the 1950s.

The Army chief of staff, on a visit to Fairbanks after World War II, took time to tee off at the Fairbanks Golf and Country Club, visit the University of Alaska, and deliver a reassuring message to a Fairbanks audience. "Ladd Field and Satellite are in a very fine area from the standpoint of weather and terrain and they must have very fine bases," Gen. Dwight D. Eisenhower said at a Ladd Field press conference. "We will not by any manner or means destroy the framework of our defensive system."

While the military pulled back elsewhere in America after the war, in Fairbanks a postwar construction boom during the Cold War led to explosive growth and drastic changes. The Satellite officially became Eielson Air Force Base in early 1948, and the base expanded to handle Strategic Air Command intercontinental bombers. At one time, Eielson had the longest runway in North America at 14,518 feet.

An Outsider's perspective came from Noel Monks, writing in the *London Daily Mail* about postwar Fairbanks in 1948. "It's ironic that this town, through which poured the American and Canadian equipment that helped the Russians to save their country, is accepted as the G.H.Q. of the early stages of the atomic war, which everyone here is convinced will come within the next five years. And who will the enemy be? 'Why, our gallant allies, the Russians, who single-handedly saved the world for democracy,' a U.S. colonel who has no illusions left, told me.

"At Twenty-Six Mile, an airfield will be completed within the next few weeks designed especially for bombers that will carry atom bombs 5,000 miles non-stop," Monks told his London readers.

In the Cold War atmosphere of Fairbanks in the 1950s, air attacks on Fairbanks were thought to be a serious enough threat to warrant practice blackouts, similar to those of a decade earlier. "With enemy action possible at any time against this city, local civil defense of the highest possible quality is of the utmost importance," said Fairbanks Civil Defense Director Evan Peterson in the spring of 1952.

During one blackout, radio announcers climbed atop the Polaris building to spot lights that were left on. "In one case, they mentioned the home of a prominent local businessman. As his wife moved from room to room, turning out lights, the announcers called her by name and complimented her," the *News-Miner* reported.

Cold War defensive measures originated with a view of Interior Alaska as a key place on the world's air routes. "The polar concept of global defense began to receive recognition and Alaska became one of the most strategic spots on earth," Richard Cooley wrote in a 1954 *Survey of Progress* about Fairbanks.

The government spent hundreds of millions of dollars on defense systems because of concerns about the Soviet threat. As a result, Fairbanks become a boom town again.

The population of the area increased by 240 percent from 1940 to 1950 and doubled between 1950 and 1953, putting an enormous strain on community facilities and triggering a retail and building boom that changed the face of the town. In two years, thirty-six new subdivisions were started in the area, and each one, according to one analyst, was "laid out at the whim of the individual plotter."

Eight hundred people waited for telephone service, schools went to double shifts, traffic jammed the Cushman Street Bridge, and old cabins disappeared so steadily that novelist Edna Ferber, while on a visit gathering material for *Ice Palace*, her novel about Alaska, recom-

The downtown swimming pool drew crowds of kids on warm summer days in the late 1940s.

mended that Fairbanks ought to be hanging onto more of those old buildings for the tourists' sake.

But there were more pressing concerns than preserving the past. These included updating the hopelessly inadequate sewer system, water system, power supply, road system, and getting modern houses built. There were only 241 water customers and the sewer system, installed in 1939, was practically useless during certain portions of the year because of the cold weather. Only two miles of the twenty-two miles of city streets were paved and only a few hundred yards of the nineteen miles of suburban streets were paved.

School enrollment grew from 560 in 1943 to 2,363 a decade later, four times as many students in three times as many classrooms. The Chamber of Commerce appealed for federal help, saying there was a "critical overloading of all our community facilities."

"Not only is the Fairbanks municipality bursting at its seams, but the outlying areas which have been settled largely by military families are completely without the facilities which every American has a right to expect," the chamber said in its appeal for assistance.

Fairbanks was a town in a hurry, impatient with the old and eager to build anew. Up until 1940, it had been an old mining camp. That changed with the war. The community wasn't planned. It just happened. And there wasn't a public facility that was adequate to handle the population growth.

Consider the city jail, known as the "black hole of Fairbanks." It had a main cell block for twelve men with one toilet and one washstand. There were usually eighteen men in jail and their food consisted of "coffee, water and one stale roll each day, augmented by one full meal a week," Richard Cooley wrote in his report on Fairbanks conditions.

The city had contained 1.3 square miles up until 1952, when the addition of the Brandt Subdivision, Mooreland Acres, and Westgate nearly doubled it to 2.4 square miles. An additional square mile was close to being annexed, but the city boundaries could never keep up with the size of the community. At least seventy percent of new houses were built outside the city.

Slaterville, Lemeta, Island Homes, Hamilton Acres, Weeks Field,

South Fairbanks, and College all showed rapid growth. There were grow-ing suburbs with modern split-levels hard by old cabins and temporary trailers that popped up in every direction.

Across the river Slaterville was home to 611 residents and Graehl had 476 residents in 1950. "Fairbanks had no suburbs 11 years ago," *Jessen's Weekly* reported in 1950. "There was not even a Slaterville, but where private homes now mushroom, there were grassy fields where large patches of red raspberries ripened and groves of spruce and birch."

Slaterville came about when Charles Slater started selling lots in his fields in 1939, when construction was getting going on Ladd Field. Earl and Pat Cook said their friends thought they were moving across the world instead of across the river by building there. "Why are you mov-ing so far out of town? We'll never see you," their friends said.

While some areas wanted to be annexed to the city, neighborhoods like Graehl put up a stubborn resistance. Almost every property owner in Graehl, the oldest Fairbanks suburb, opposed annexation in 1961. "You speak of water pollution," Graehl resident Fabian Carey said at an annexation hearing. "In all my time in Graehl I have known of several cases of alcohol poisoning, but never a case of typhoid fever."

The traffic pattern in Graehl, Slaterville, and Fairbanks changed in 1953 with the completion of the first new bridges since horse and buggy days, the Wendell Street Bridge over the Chena and the Minnie Street Bridge over Noyes Slough. Opening the bridges eased congestion on the Cushman Street Bridge, traffic on which was thereafter restricted to vehicles under five tons. The new bridges allowed easier access from the fast-growing suburbs to downtown.

In the years after the war, construction increased to meet pent-up de-mand. "Housing was short and you could sell anything," said Cook, a pio-neer real estate agent. On one occasion Cook showed a house for sale to two colonels from Ladd. They came back to his office at the same time and both wanted to buy the house. They flipped a coin to determine the winner.

The Joesting homestead was bought by the Westfair Corp., which started the Westgate Subdivision, and would-be homeowners snapped up half the lots in a matter of months. The Aurora subdivision, pur-chased from homesteader L.T. Hilling in 1949, was starting to draw resi-

UAF Archives

Downtown Fairbanks remained the city's commercial center in the 1950s with a variety of shops and stores catering to the needs of the rapidly growing population

dents, with some lots available for $450. "We are attempting to bridge the Noyes Slough from Aurora to the College Road," said boxer-turned-realtor Bud Meyeres in 1952. Lots were still available in Lemeta, the former homestead that took its name from the first two letters of the last names of developers Gradelle Leigh, Bud Meyeres, and Warren Taylor.

C.H. Sullivan, known as the "Smiling Irishman," was developing the Bjerremark homestead, a 150-acre site west of Cushman from 19th to 30th Avenues. "He reports that most of the temporary streets have been brushed out and some are completed," the *News-Miner* said in its *1952 Progress Edition.*

A crash building program over two years helped relieve the housing shortage with the construction of: Queens Court, Dixon Apartments, Fairview Manor, Northward Building, Birch Park, Polaris Building, Hamilton Apartments, Island Homes, Arctic Park, and Mooreland Courts.

Out of town, the Golden Valley Electric Association provided power to 2,000 customers in 1954. It had started in the 1940s when homesteaders and farmers got together to try to get power lines to rural areas. In 1953, the association bought the old FE Co. power plant. "We'll not be satisfied until we serve all the farmers and homesteaders in the valley," said Nick Eidem, GVEA manager. "We are working toward the time when we can introduce a rate structure for electricity that will encourage the use of sprinkle irrigation."

The coming of electricity would help bring back agriculture, promoters said, and "with electricity in rural homes, the number of families moving to town for the winter will decrease. It will be practical to live in the country the year-round as soon as the 'electrical hired man' is on the job. With children of school age living in the rural areas, some school buses will be operated. Gradually the small dot of civilization on the map of the Interior will start to grow."

Someday, GVEA founders hoped, "the entire Farmers Loop will be built up with farms and suburban homes." Major GVEA customers in the early days included the radio station KFRB—the second radio station in Fairbanks—Creamer's Dairy, and the Geophysical Institute at the university.

Writer Herb Hilscher said Alaska newspapers "just about missed the boat" by downplaying the news of the institute's creation in 1948 through a bill signed by President Harry Truman. Hilscher predicted that one day the Geophysical Institute would be to scientific study in the arctic what MIT was to engineering and Harvard was to business.

"The Geophysical Institute, under inspired leadership, can roll back the mysteries of the largest unexplored areas left in our world," Hilscher wrote. "It can attract outstanding scholars to its research staff. It can draw these men from many countries. Science knows no nationalistic boundaries, and leading professors from all over the globe can gather here to study Arctic phenomena."

National boundaries and the need to defend them, however, prompted the federal government to spend more than $250 million on base construction at Ladd and Eielson from 1950 to 1955. Added to this was a $40 million annual payroll.

A Town Transformed

This financial windfall opened a new era in Fairbanks, just as the railroad and the FE Co. had a quarter-century earlier. There were 462 federal employees in the Fairbanks area and 191 territorial employees. Of the 220 business establishments in 1950, 115 had union contracts.

"Business has boomed," Richard Cooley wrote in 1954. "Hundreds of new retail and service needs are being provided which formerly could only be obtained Outside. Many of the businesses presently related to and dependent upon military construction are developing into permanent establishments."

The military boom town had just about swallowed the old Weeks Field airport and the air carriers were flying into a new $5 million airport built by the federal government six miles from the town. The 6,000-foot runway was open and in use before city authorities shut down Weeks Field on Oct. 15, 1951. The closure of Weeks Field was timed to coincide with the opening of the new Denali Elementary School, which was next to the runway.

Operators, who objected to the high price of moving to the new airport and the lack of facilities, said they should be allowed to continue using Weeks Field. Two men made protest landings after a red cross was painted on the strip to show it was closed and they found themselves under arrest. "The school building is no closer to the runway than the control tower; yet to the best of our knowledge no planes have hit the control tower," Weeks Field proponents said. Some of them moved their operations to the new Phillips Field airport, a small airfield that operated for more than three decades and was later paved over by the Johansen Expressway.

After the closure of Weeks Field, new and larger aircraft soon began flying into Fairbanks International Airport. In time, Pan American replaced some of its DC-4s with pressurized DC-6s, which reduced the flying time to Seattle from eight hours to six hours. The old Pan American hangar at Weeks Field became the center of the Arctic Bowl building. Rows of new houses were built nearby and the airstrip began to disappear, part of it becoming a park and in 1977, the home of the community library.

There were other changes in transportation as well. Eight taxi com-

Bernie Rinear

One of the most popular places to watch the end of the three-day North American Champion-ship sled dog race in 1948 was near the parimutual betting booth.

panies with a total of sixty cabs roamed the streets, few of which were paved in the early 1950s. During the winter, the cabs ran twenty-four hours a day and each one carried an average of eighty persons per day. At that pace the typical cab lasted a year on the streets of Fairbanks. The increasing use of car engine heaters in the 1950s led to a decline in taxi numbers and an increased number of private cars operating year-round.

A major program in 1953 to put a hard surface on thirty-three blocks of streets downtown was plagued by problems blamed on the contractor's reliance on a 1909 city survey that didn't match the way the roads had been built. In 1909, it was said, the city used "shovel handles" to measure distance. The most impressive new building on the six-mile-long Airport Road was the big Lathrop High School, named for Alaska's richest man, who died in 1950 when he fell beneath the wheels of a loaded coal car at his mine in Healy. The downtown skyline was dominated by the two tallest buildings ever to be constructed in Fairbanks. Referred to at the time as "skyscrapers," the green two-tone 100-foot-high Polaris Building and the eight-story Northward Building, which gleamed in the sun, were symbols of community pride.

Second Avenue, where parking meters were installed in 1948, remained the town's commercial center. Traffic lights started making their appearance, beginning with one at the corner of Second and Cushman. The Chena building, home of the Chena Department Store, was built on a site formerly occupied by the Peerless Coffee Shop. Peerless, a landmark in its day, had a copper coffee pot that looked like a reformed still. "It gives forth husky coffee that will nearly float a horseshoe," a coffee aficionado claimed.

The NC whistle, which called people to work and announced noon for decades, sounded for the last time in May 1952. Jesse Rust, a long-time employee, pulled the cord for the final blast. About that time the First National Bank installed a time and temperature sign, which became one of Fairbanks' most photographed landmarks. That year marked the third for the *Godspeed*, a riverboat Jim and Mary Binkley offered to give tourists an extended tour of the Chena and Tanana Rivers.

Shortly after the new airport became operational, Scandinavian Airlines System stopped in Fairbanks during an over-the-pole test flight from Europe to Asia. Fairbanks tried but failed to beat out Anchorage as the Alaska stop for the passenger flights that followed.

Employment in Fairbanks skyrocketed by 100 percent in five years, but the unemployment rate rose as well because hundreds of new workers arrived every spring to look for work. Seasonal arrivals had three big problems: no money, no place to stay, and no chance to find the high-paying jobs they had dreamed of. People slept in basements, hallways, back seats of cars, trailer camps, cabins, and wanigans. Some barely had enough money to scrape by.

Gold mining, which had been the lifeblood of Fairbanks in the 1930s, staged a brief comeback after the war, but inflation and the fixed $35 price of gold led the industry downward toward obscurity. One FE Co. postwar employee was Niilo Koponen, who had been born in the Bronx in 1928 and came north with his wife Joan to homestead. "We used to call it the 'school of hard knocks' and said everybody had to 'graduate' from the FE Co.," Koponen, a future teacher and state legislator, told artist Jean Lester. "It was hard and dirty but working on the line crew and the electric crew both, I got out to every one of the dredges and dredge camps."

Although mining was greatly diminished from what it had been, Fairbanks started its annual Golden Days celebration to remember the town's historic past. The Secretary of the Interior was the first guest of honor and the Fairbanks Chamber of Commerce invited President Eisenhower to preside at the second Golden Days celebration, but he declined.

Fairbanks was an active town in the 1950s, with more than 100 lodges, clubs, and other groups such as the Burnt Toastmasters Club, a dozen labor unions, thirty churches, six PTAs, homemaker clubs, Take Off Pounds Sensibly club, American Legion, Curling Club, Kennel Club, two Ski Clubs, Arctic Amateur Radio Club, Soroptimists, Moose, Lions, Eagles, American Legion, Elks, Rotary, Chamber of Commerce, Jaycees, Odd Fellows, Pioneers, Kiwanis, Rebekahs, Quota, Boy Scouts, Girl Scouts, and the Masons.

In mid-decade television brought a major change. Territorial legislator and insurance man John Butrovich gave city firemen a new TV set on Christmas Eve 1954, six weeks before the first local station, KTVF Channel 11, went on the air. Its first program—other than a test pattern that was shown for thirty minutes and a dedication program—was "The Life of Riley." President of Northern Television was Augie Hiebert, the former KFAR engineer who had been the first to sound the alarm in Fairbanks about the attack on Pearl Harbor.

KTVF was followed on the air by KFAR-TV a couple of weeks later. That station, run by Al Bramstedt, who had worked with Hiebert at KFAR radio, opened its operations with a dedication program of hula dancing, tap dancing, violin playing, and speeches, followed by a presentation of the "This is Your Life" episode devoted to Eva McGown, the hostess of Fairbanks. There were only about 400 TV sets in Fairbanks when the stations went on the air, but stores were selling more fast. Nerland's advertised a twenty-one-inch Philco "Double Door Console" in "lustrous mahogany" for $369.95.

Ellen Whitcher, society editor of the *News-Miner*, wrote a couple of years later that television had "done a lot to combat cabin fever and winter doldrums, but doesn't help on those mornings when the thermometer shows a cool fifty degrees below zero, the ice fog hides the house next door and nothing seems to be moving but the tow trucks and taxis." ∎

UAF Archives / Griffin Collection

The Cushman Street bridge was a focal point for many activities in the community including the annual breakup betting pools and dog sled races on the frozen river.

Fairbanks Daily News-Miner

The University of Alaska underwent dramatic growth after World War II.

Playing on the Frozen Tundra

Football fans know the Rose, Sugar, Cotton, Fiesta, Orange, and other bowl games that feature the best of the college game. But few know that Fairbanks had its own New Year's Day game—the Ice Bowl. The Ice Bowl originated when a University of Alaska student sports writer and another scribe from the Ladd Field newspaper complained in late 1948 about the lack of college football in Fairbanks. "From there, the two conceived of the 'Ice Bowl' to be played on New Year's Day between Ladd Field's football team, the Ladd Flyers, and the university," Neil Davis, a retired UA scientist, wrote. "That the university had no football team was a minor detail, the two reasoned. They were right. The idea was so far off the wall that it appealed to many male students who, at this time of year, were as bored as the instigators."

Thirty-five students, nearly twenty percent of the male enrollment, signed up for the impromptu team two weeks before the big game, set for January 1, 1949. Only one player had any college football experience and about half had never played the game competitively. Expecting normal January weather, players planned to dress in whatever pads they could borrow along with mukluks, scarves, and mittens. It was thirty below on game day. "At the temperature pertaining that day, the pigskin had a resiliency and texture similar to that of steel," Davis wrote in his book *The College Hill Chronicles.* "If a quarterback could manage to throw the ball, a receiver could not catch it." Ice Bowl I ended in a 0-0 tie, which the university took as a victory, having expected to lose to the Air Force.

The buildup for Ice Bowl II included publication of a thirty-eight page program. Fairbanks never had a Tournament of Roses Parade, but Ice Bowl II featured a half-time show that included Ice Bowl Queen Susie Williams circling the field on a dog sled. One of the fans in attendance was Alaska Gov. Ernest Gruening, who called it the "farthest north gridiron championship in the world." The first half ended in a 0-0 tie, but in the second half Leo Helsby, No. 39, kicked a field goal, the only points ever scored for the university in an Ice Bowl. It was enough to give the students a 3-0 win.

By Ice Bowl III, player turnout was so poor that the UA coach decided that he couldn't go through with the game; ten players were not enough. Most UA students, Davis wrote in his book, "did not care diddly-squat one way or the other about varsity athletics." The students insisted on playing the game, however, and they drafted a couple of visitors to Fairbanks to join them and had them play under the names of UA students. The team had three offensive plays, one to the right, one to the left, and one to the middle.

For Ice Bowl III, the twelve UA players wore several pairs of socks and had chicken wire wrapped around their tennis shoes for more traction. The Ladd players did not have chicken wire on their feet, but they had fifty-six players and the team had recently won the Pacific Theater military championship. Still, it was never easy to score when the field was covered with snow, and Ice Bowl III went into the books as another tie.

Ice Bowl IV, the last in the series, was played in 1952. The Ladd Flyers scored on the second play of the game and kept on scoring on their way to a cool 47-0 whitewash. Dean Neil Hosley offered post-game analysis: "I think this should show our boys the days of picking up a handful of players the last minute and tying or winning the Ice Bowl are gone."

The days of the Ice Bowl were gone too. ■

A Bridge to the Future

For many years a sign near the Cushman Street Bridge warned: "Speed Limit 6 Miles per Hour. Walk Your Horses." The sign was gone by 1948, but the bridge was hopelessly out of date, the principal factor that started what some people called the "Battle of the Bridge."

The only bridge across the Chena River carried 4,500 cars a day, but it was too narrow for trucks and buses, which straddled the center. This led to showdowns with drivers who thought trucks and buses shouldn't be taking up both lanes. Bus owner Paul Greimann said it was entirely a safety issue. A combative young man named Joe Vogler, who would be involved in many confrontations with the authorities over the next four decades, went to court in 1948 seeking a permanent injunction against straddling the center line.

Several times a bus going one way and a car or truck going the other way attempted crossing the bridge at the same time. On several occasions, neither would back off to allow the other to pass; they sat in a stalemate with both engines growling. Vogler was one of several people who challenged the bus company. Traffic tie-ups ended with police sometimes issuing tickets to both drivers or threatening to get a tow truck to remove the bus.

The buses and trucks continued straddling the center line for several more years, but if nothing else, the bridge battles illustrated the need for a new bridge. Opening the Wendell Street Bridge in 1953 eased the problem, but a new Cushman Street Bridge, hailed as a "Span of Progress," didn't open until 1960. "Gone are the ugly, narrow girders, and the tunnellike darkness which was such a problem in the winter," the *News-Miner* said. "In the place of that old eyesore structure has been built a new bridge pleasing to look at and functional."

The old bridge had more life left in it; it was taken to Nome, where it is still used. A Cushman Street Bridge sign remains on the bridge, which now crosses a small river on a lonely road outside of Nome. When the steel bridge was completed in 1917, it had been hailed as a span of progress too. "We are thankful to all who helped to give us this fine bridge and now we can stand in the middle of it when the ice is going out and laugh at Nature's fury," the high school students declared in their 1917 annual.

The bridge played a part in determining the exact time of breakup in the Chena, which was important because bets were placed on the matter in almost every cigar store and hotel. Cafe owner Arthur Williams and R.J. Sommers felt a precise method was needed. They first said that when their flagpole passed under the steel bridge that would be the breakup. A pole with the name of one or more businesses on it was planted in the ice and when it hit the steel bridge, it would trigger a clock. Eddie Suter suggested a clock to stop the bickering about the exact minute the ice went out.

"The ice move has always been used to advertise some concern in town and sometimes two or more concerns and the usual time disputes are apt to be on again this year," a reporter said. "Some of them don't want the official time registered by electricity unless it is their time."

Getting a bridge built across the Chena Slough had took years. About fifteen temporary bridges were built over the years; the wooden bridges were destroyed almost every spring by the breakup, which sent massive chunks of ice downstream. Every spring volunteers gathered just before breakup and salvaged what they could so it could be reused in a new bridge. An annual competition developed among waterfront businesses about exactly where the bridge would be built; all wanted to be close to it. Usually the bridge was built at Turner Street next to the NC Co., the biggest business in town.

Congressional delegate James Wickersham claimed it had taken so long for a permanent bridge because the NC Co. wanted the bridge left at Turner Street by the NC complex. Wickersham disliked Col. Wilds Richardson, head of the Alaska Road Commission, and said Richardson would never agree to build the bridge until told to by the NC Co. He said that Richardson was "viciously incompetent" and "under the control of the Northern Commercial Co."

The enmity between the two was demonstrated when Richardson called Wickersham "a scurrilous, political blatherskite, permanently afflicted with about every phase of mental perversion and a complete moral idiocy." It was Wickersham who backed legislation specifying the bridge was to be built "across the Chena River where the present military and post road reaches the same, and connecting the said road from the north end of Cushman Street." ∎

14

Celebrating Statehood

UAF Archives / Rivers Collection

William Egan, future governor of Alaska, signs his name to the Alaska state constitution, written at the University of Alaska during the winter of 1955-56 by fifty-five delegates.

On the last day of June 1958, the Chena River flowed fluorescent green through the middle of Fairbanks. It was all a mistake. The idea had been to color the river bright gold, befitting a Golden Heart City celebration of Congressional approval of statehood for Alaska.

Celebrating Statehood

The attempt at alchemy reflected the eagerness and excitement with which many Alaskans awaited statehood, an attitude that has long since vanished from the political scene. Congressional passage of statehood fulfilled a long-sought dream that symbolized progress and freedom to Alaskans in the 1950s. After approval by Congress, the president signed the bill and later that summer Alaskans endorsed statehood by a vote of 40,452 to 8,010. Alaska officially became the 49th state on Jan. 3, 1959.

The new star on the flag ended a long campaign of reformers and activists who believed that statehood would give Alaskans greater control over their destiny and end federal domination of their affairs. Proponents looked forward to gaining two senators and a representative in Congress, the chance to vote in presidential elections and status as a full partner in the American experience. In the decades that followed, the goal of local control never quite lived up to the rhetoric, because the federal government remained the largest

Fairbanks Daily News-Miner

Delegates to the Alaska Constitutional Convention discuss some of the fine points of drafting a governmental blueprint for Alaska before the television cameras in Fairbanks.

landholder, controlling about two-thirds of the land in the 49th state.

On the day of final passage of the statehood bill by the Senate, the last real test of the measure, the publisher of the *News-Miner*, C.W. Snedden kept a phone line open from Washington, D.C., and conveyed the news in mid-afternoon on June 30, 1958.

After the Senate voted 64-20 to accept Alaska, fire and civil defense sirens sounded in the summer afternoon air, attracting crowds downtown along the Chena River. A crew directed by George Huber launched a thirty-foot gold star with the number "49" sewn on. Carried aloft by weather balloons and secured by guy wires, the forty-ninth star rose in the sky. The star flew until just before midnight, when it dipped between the Polaris and Northward buildings and caught on a power line, triggering a power outage. The sixteen-minute power failure did not sap the energy of the statehood celebration that continued long into the night.

Promoter Don Pearson headed the project to make the Chena flow gold, adding dye the Air Force normally used during rescues at sea. A local sportsman mentioned that there was no need to worry about harming the fish in the river. "The Chena River is not the finest, purest stream in the country, not with all that sewage being dumped in it," he said. Pearson's crew dumped the bags of dye, enough to color almost a two-acre area, from the Wendell Street Bridge. Apparently the dye turned salt water gold and fresh water green, leading one witness to say, "Green gold is better than none."

A year later, long after the Chena had returned to a darker shade of green, Fairbanks recreated the statehood celebration with a parade that turned into a real Hollywood production. A crew from Warner Brothers filmed a reenactment of the statehood celebration for scenes in the movie *Ice Palace*. The novel of the same name by Edna Ferber had helped popularize the cause of Alaska statehood in the United States.

The novel featured the fictional coastal town of Baranof, a community that otherwise resembled Fairbanks, with midnight summer baseball games, a winter festival, a couple of shiny new apartment buildings, old log cabins, gold dredges outside of town, and two nearby military bases. Ferber based Bridie Ballantyne, the official greeter of the city, on

Eva McGown, while she loosely based Czar Kennedy, the white-haired millionaire who died after having been run over by a coal car at his mine, on Cap Lathrop.

The part of the movie filmed in Fairbanks included a few exterior shots of the Northward Building, the model of the Ice Palace, some scenes taken at the airport, and a downtown parade that drew 1,000 people. "It was better than last year," one resident said. Movie star Robert Ryan, who played the pro-statehood character Thor Storm, rode in a convertible and a military band marched along with flag-waving Boy Scouts, veterans, average citizens, children, babies, and dogs. Unfortunately, the parade scene wound up on the cutting room floor, leaving the June 30, 1958 celebration as the only one to remember.

Leading up to the statehood celebrations, one of the major turning points in the campaign occurred in Fairbanks in 1955-56 when fifty-five men and women, the same number of delegates who wrote the United States Constitution, gathered at the University of Alaska to draft a constitution for the future state. The Alaska delegates, selected in elections throughout the territory, included thirteen lawyers, two ministers, two pilots, four miners, twenty-one businessmen, three fishermen, six professionals, three housewives, and one homesteader. Eight had been born in the Territory and Tlingit Indian Frank Peratrovich, a Klawock merchant, was the only Alaska Native. There were forty-nine men and six women in the group.

The Fairbanks weather emerged as one of the unique "unifying influences" on the constitution creators, recalled delegate and historian Victor Fischer. The convention opened in November, with the temperature at sixteen below, and the weather bottomed out at fifty-three below before the proceedings ended the following February.

Near midnight on January 25, during an intense session on the declaration of rights section, Convention President Bill Egan warned that the temperature had dropped outside the hall. "The Chair would like to announce that the temperature is now about 40 below and if the delegates have their cars out there, they probably should start them in order that they will start," Egan said. After giving their cars a chance to warm up, the delegates returned to a debate that was

Jeff Studdert hooks sixty-seven dogs to his sled at the site of the Alaska 67 Exposition, now known as Alaskaland, in 1967 to mark the centennial of the purchase of Alaska.

noticeably cooler, Fischer wrote in his history of the convention.

The campus location proved ideal for the task. Isolation allowed delegates to escape the lobbying pressures that would have prevailed in Juneau and helped create a sense of detachment about the undertaking. The delegates did most of their work in the campus building that had been renamed Constitution Hall. They decided how to structure the branches of government and to divide powers and responsibilities, drafting a document that would win praise as a model for the future state, and that has required relatively few changes over the years.

With the work completed, Egan, the convention leader who became Alaska's first elected governor, signed the governmental framework first. He shook so hard as he wrote his name that he finally dropped the pen in disgust while "others who followed were equally as overcome by the moment," the *News-Miner* reported.

When Alaska entered the union, Fairbanks leaders hoped that an economy long dependent on military spending might soon find a more secure foundation. A vice president of the Alaska National Bank summed up the dependence in the late 1950s when he said of the Army and Air Force, "We need you as our biggest and almost only customer."

In time, the banks had more customers in part because of a key economic provision in the statehood act that gave Alaska the right to select 103 million acres of federally-owned land for state owner- ship. The most important selections made under that authority cov- ered 1.8 million acres on the North Slope. No rock outcroppings on the swampy surface hinted at huge oil deposits two miles under- ground, but geologists detected similarities in the underground rock structures with the oil-bearing regions of the Rockies. The state re- ceived tentative approval to the land in 1964, a small part of which would prove to hold the largest oil field in North America.

Even before the oil boom revolutionized the Fairbanks economy in the 1970s, the community continued to expand, supported by the military, the university, and a growing tourism industry. "Modern, well-built homes are increasing both in the city and in several of the good surrounding subdivisions," realtor Bud Meyeres said in 1963. "Now in keeping with the general growth of the area, new homes are being built on the spacious, sunny southern slopes of the hills so close to central Fairbanks."

The business section, which had long been confined to a space of several blocks on the river front, began to spread. "For the first time in the history of the city," Mayor Darrell Brewington said in 1963 after the paving of Noble Street and other improvements, "a motorist can drive along the streets of the central downtown area without weaving curb to curb dodging chuck holes." It was also possible by then to walk from Gaffney Road to downtown on sidewalks instead of dirt paths.

In 1940, a critic said that aside from the federal building, the Lacey Street Theater, and the Lathrop Building, the rest of the town's homes and businesses generally follow the "architectural pattern of the Leaning Tower of Pisa and include a hump or a wave or two in the middle." Leaning towers remained in Fairbanks two decades later, but their numbers had dwindled.

The most often asked question about the new Foodland Shopping Center that opened in 1960 was "Why is it round?" The same was asked about the new school in Lemeta named for electrician and longtime school board member Louis Joy. In each case, the answer was that circular buildings were deemed to be more efficient and modern. "The advanced circular design allows a more convenient access to each classroom," the school district proclaimed about Joy Elementary School.

Transportation improvements made it more convenient for travelers to get to the Lower 48 and back. On March 1, 1960, Pan American inaugurated civilian passenger jet service with a Boeing 707 flight from Seattle to Fairbanks and back. The flight didn't land at Fairbanks International Airport, however, because the 6,000-foot runway was about a half-mile shorter than the Ladd Field runway. The Air Force gave temporary permission for jet flights to land at Ladd and some Washington officials suggested the long-term use of Ladd for commercial jets.

The tenor of the discussion changed, however, when the Air Force announced that it would be shutting down Ladd Field for good and concentrating its forces at Eielson Air Force Base. "We're sure that the decision to rub out air defenses in the heart of Alaska is being viewed with satisfaction in Moscow today," the *News-Miner* said in a front-page editorial headlined "Red Tape; Black Crepe." The clamor over the shutdown subsided when the Army announced that it would move troops from Eielson and elsewhere to Ladd and rename the facility for Jonathan M. Wainwright, a World War II hero.

At the start, many Alaskans thought of statehood in political and economic terms and speculated on how it would influence government and speed progress. Some people, however, wondered about the social consequences. Joan Koponen, a Fairbanks homesteader, said she hoped that statehood would not "tame" Alaska and bring an end to the qualities that made it attractive. "Many of us, almost all, traveled the thousands of miles to reach a country where each man seemed to count for more and where convention and all the petty social pressures counted for a little less than in the States," she wrote at the end of the statehood fight. "I hope this will not be the good-bye to the untamed and the lone spirit that is so much here, often daredevil and independent and not caring a hoot about conformity," she said. "People will flock here because it is now a good respectable state.

"To drive around Fairbanks—what a marvelous collection of people daring to live as they want to live—everything from hair styles to houses," Koponen said.

In the years since statehood, Fairbanks has become much more like communities elsewhere because of a rising standard of living and improved technology and community facilities. The typical Fairbanks resident lives in a home that wouldn't look out of place anywhere in the United States. Myths about "rugged individualism" being a hallmark of

Fairbanks Daily News-Miner

The E.T. Barnette cabin, one of the oldest relics of early Fairbanks, was torn down in the late 1950s. The urge to get rid of old buildings and replace them with newer ones has long been a community trait.

the populace retain a hold on the imagination, but there are still non-conformists who call Fairbanks home, daring to live as they choose. The community still has unique characteristics, mainly due to weather and geography, yet the forces of social and economic change set in motion by the statehood act continue.

In the years that followed, differences between Fairbanks and small towns in the Lower 48 diminished, especially as new community facilities, improved transportation, and communications advancements combined to lessen the isolation that some people craved and others loathed. By the end of the 1960s, technology had advanced to the point that live television coverage of the Apollo 11 landing on the moon could be beamed to Anchorage by way of a military satellite. A group of Fairbanksans flew to Anchorage that day so they could watch Neil Armstrong's giant leap for mankind live. Fairbanks witnessed some live coverage of a later Apollo mission, but most of the first live TV broadcasts featured major football games, which in the past had been shown days or weeks after the fact. Fairbanks tuned in for its first satellite sports broadcast when the Miami Dolphins met the Pittsburgh Steelers in the December 1972 AFC Championship game.

Of all the changes that occurred in Fairbanks, however, between statehood and the oil boom, none surpassed the events of August 1967, when the gentle river that had once been dyed bright green turned into a deadly torrent. ■

Symphony of Sounds

The first announcement, dated January 14, 1959, began with an exclamation: "Fairbanks is going to have a symphony orchestra!"

Brought together by Lathrop High School band director Jack Lind, the assembled musicians wondered, however, if they would have enough string players to create the right sound. "Lind stated that the symphony could only be a success if every available string player in the entire area wanted to participate," the symphony planners said. "If the string players show up, Fairbanks is on its way to a symphony."

One of those who showed up was violinist Angela Teegardin. One of eighteen violinists who played in the first concert given by the Fairbanks Symphony Orchestra, Teegardin and the other string players performed May 3, 1959, in the new Hunter School multipurpose room. When not playing music, the orchestra members could be found throughout the community as sign painters, railroad workers, students, housewives, and military personnel.

The concert site had been picked in late April after the fifty-one musicians in the orchestra tested the acoustics of the room at Hunter. It sounded as good or better there any other place in the Fairbanks area. At its first concert, the orchestra played eight selections, including *The Winter of the Blue Snow*, based on the winter during Paul Bunyan's time when it was so cold all the loggers "swore a blue streak."

Today, the volunteer symphony has about seventy members, musicians who represent a cross-section of the community and know that joining the group is a commitment to "practice on Tuesday night for the rest of your life," except in the summer. Through its first four decades, Teegardin never missed a year with the volunteer symphony, an organization that established itself as a musical mainstay in Fairbanks.

Other names of note who participated in that first symphony concert, who remained active in the Fairbanks music scene into the late 1990s, were Fred Brown, Peggy Swartz, Gerald Grill, and Lesley Salisbury. Given special attention on the program for the first concert was "Conductor Aide" Chuck Rees, who helped with the logistics. ∎

New Era for Alaska Natives

Renewed controversy over the long-neglected land rights of Alaska's Native population emerged following the approval of the Alaska Statehood Act, precipitating major changes for Alaska's Native people.

Alaska Natives made up about one-fifth of the population at the time of statehood, most living in about two hundred villages spread across a broad expanse of rural Alaska. For the villagers, the building of the Alaska Highway and World War II brought the recognition that Alaska's first residents didn't have the full control over the land that they had always assumed they had. Natives had

UAF Archives / Bunnell Collection

The Tanana Chiefs met in Fairbanks in 1915 with James Wickersham, the first meeting dealing with land rights of Alaska's first residents. The issue of land ownership rights remained unsettled until just prior to the trans-Alaska pipeline in the 1970s.

never entered into treaties giving up their land, however, and while Congress had said as early as 1884 that these land rights were valid, no details were settled.

A proposal by the state to select land for a recreation area near Minto, northwest of Fairbanks, and talk of future oil and gas development drew protests from the villagers, who saw a direct threat to their way of life. "Claims were laid by the state on what the Minto people basically thought was their aboriginal hunting and fishing areas," Native leader Morris Thompson said. "This was the first real kind of conflict between the state of Alaska and the people of Minto and the Native community in general."

Soon other villages also protested to the Interior Department and successfully petitioned the government for a halt in the approval of land transfers to the state. The "land freeze" was to continue until Native land rights had been settled. Alfred Ketzler of Nenana and others argued that Congress needed to act decisively. "Our right to inherit land from our fathers cannot be settled in court," he said. "It is specifically stated in early laws that Congress is to do this by defining the way which we can acquire title."

Meanwhile, the *Tundra Times*, a Fairbanks-based newspaper, grew into a statewide voice for the growing political consciousness of Alaska Natives. The Alaska Federation of Natives organized, allowing groups from across the state to act in unison as they pressed their claims for land. "A lobbying effort was organized that in my view the likes of which will never be seen again," said Thompson, future president of Doyon Ltd. "It was a totally grassroots effort."

Conflicts with the state continued to escalate for several years, reaching a peak with a showdown over the plan to build the trans-Alaska pipeline. In 1970, five villages went to court to stop the pipeline permit. The politics soon became clear: To get the pipeline built, Native land claims had to be settled first. This produced the scenario needed for the state, oil companies, Native leaders, the Nixon administration, and Congress to negotiate a settlement. The Alaska Native Claims Settlement Act, approved in 1971, provided for the payment of $962.5 million, the transfer of 44 million acres of land, and the creation of 13 regional corporations.

Fairbanks became the headquarters of one of the thirteen, Doyon, Ltd. With a land entitlement of 12.5 million acres, Doyon became the largest private land owner in North America. It has 14,000 shareholders, many of whom live in villages across the Interior, and runs various enterprises including a subsidiary that operates oil drilling rigs on the North Slope.

A second regional Native organization based in Fairbanks that has also grown substantially over the years is the nonprofit Tanana Chiefs Conference, which operates a variety of federal and state-funded human services for the villages. With a work force of more than 500, TCC ranked as the 36th largest employer in Alaska in the late 1990s.

In the 1980 census, Alaska Natives made up about six percent of the population of the Fairbanks North Star Borough. A decade later the figure reached seven percent, the same as the percentage of Blacks living in the borough. ∎

The blanket toss is one of the most popular features of the World Eskimo-Indian Olympics, a summer event in Fairbanks that showcases traditional Native Alaskan sports.

15

A River Runs Through It

Bureau of Land Management

The site of the Alaska 67 Exposition, since renamed Alaskaland, was inundated by the high waters of the raging Chena and Tanana Rivers in 1967.

Sam White, a former game warden and pioneer bush pilot, marked the following words on the door of his cabin at 902 Kellum Street in August 1967: "Through this house runs the deepest river in the world."

To White and the thousands of others drying out after battling the ravages of the Chena River in 1967, it certainly seemed that way.

After a weekend of heavy rain drenched the semiarid reaches of Interior Alaska, the normally placid Chena escaped its banks and flowed through the city, flooding streets, houses, and businesses in the worst natural disaster in the town's history. The flood caused four deaths in Fairbanks, about $85 million in property damage, and forced the evacuation of about 15,000 people. "Very few of us were fortunate enough to escape without damage. Some were hit worse than others, but we all stood up, pulled ourselves together and refused to give up—we're Alaskans," said Civil Defense Director Jack Murphy.

On Monday, August 14, the Chena reached flood stage, but no one guessed the scope of the disaster to come because of the lack of river monitoring equipment upstream. "We knew it was rising quickly but we had no way of telling how high it would crest without data from upstream," said Jim Meckel, the engineer in charge of the state's water resources division. Over the weekend, Carl Wilson, the owner of Chena Hot Springs, more than sixty miles from Fairbanks, had struggled to get in touch with the city by radio to warn that the river was on a rampage, but he failed to make contact with anyone. "The flood was ripping the upper country apart and that it would serve Fairbanks the same way was a foregone conclusion," Wilson said later.

Early Monday parts of the city began to flood, forcing the evacuation of Island Homes and causing a shutdown of the A-67 exposition site celebrating the centennial of Alaska's purchase from Russia. For a decade, Fairbanks pioneers had worked to create the park that eventually became Alaskaland, which featured historic cabins, one of the last of the great sternwheelers, a domed pavilion that symbolized a gold nugget, mining equipment, exhibits of Native culture, airplanes, and other attractions. Vice President Hubert Humphrey visited the park in July while on a seven-hour stopover in Fairbanks and tried his hand at gold panning in the Mining Valley. "Let me at that," Humphrey had said. "We need some gold in Washington."

The golden hopes for the summer exposition had been dampened by lower-than-expected attendance and persistent financial problems, but on August 14, the flood made the earlier worries seem trifling. As the river rose, it washed out part of the small railroad that circled the park. The water eventually came within six inches of the *Big Stampede* murals created by artist Rusty Heurlin and covered the stage in the Civic Center and the first seven rows of seats.

Volunteers, some of whom became stranded at the site, moved millions of dollars worth of exhibits, displays, and paintings to keep them dry. One ham radio operator, James "Mac" McGuire, set up his station in the wheelhouse of the sternwheeler *Nenana*, and contacted radio stations throughout the United States with news of the flood. Drains in the *Nenana* had been opened to flood the cargo deck of the sternwheeler and keep it from floating away.

Bureau of Land Management

The Chena and Tanana rivers overflowed their banks in August 1967, causing millions of dollars of damage and forcing thousands to flee to higher ground.

The upper decks of the *Nenana* remained high and dry, but it was not so easy to protect St. Joseph's Hospital upstream from the Cushman Street Bridge. Sister Conrad Mary, St. Joseph's administrator, watched the river climb about six inches every hour Monday afternoon. "Early in the afternoon sand bags were dumped at our door," she said. "Literally hundreds of people came to help and quickly a three-foot high sand bag dike was erected all around the hospital."

For a while the dike was almost waterproof, but the river rose with a relentless force that surpassed the fourteen major floods that had occurred since 1905. That night Governor Wally Hickel declared Fairbanks a disaster area. City Mayor H.A. "Red" Boucher and Civil Defense Director Murphy advised evacuating the hospital patients and taking them to Bassett Army Hospital on Fort Wainwright.

Nurses and nuns made adhesive tape markers to place on the patients' foreheads before ambulances, taxis, and private cars evacuated the sick. The last patient departed shortly before high water closed the Cushman Street Bridge. A pedestrian recalled that the bridge shook as huge chunks of debris smashed into it from beneath.

"Something sure as heck must have happened between 9:30 and midnight last night," Hickel said the next morning, after the river had risen to more than eighteen feet, three feet higher than the flood forecasts. "I didn't realize things were this bad. It's a disaster."

By foot, car, boat, truck, and helicopter, people fled homes by the thousands, taking refuge at the University of Alaska, Lathrop High School, Eielson Air Force Base, Main School, and other evacuation centers, escaping water that typically ranged from knee-deep to chest-high. In some spots the water ran nine feet deep.

Margaret Ofstad saw a man clinging to the top of the revolving door of the Northward Building. The man had to jump and swim to a rescue boat, which could get no closer than fifteen feet because of the current. Bassett Army Hospital at Fort Wainwright remained open, but the basement flooded, knocking out power, which forced doctors and nurses to deliver several babies by flashlight.

The Binkley family, operators of the Riverboat *Discovery*, stayed on their tourist boat after their home flooded, though it was a round-the-clock job to keep the riverboat from being swept away. In the meantime, radio broadcasters Bill "Wee Willie" Walley, Maury Smith, Bob Parsons, and others at KFAR stayed on the air with twenty-four-hour flood coverage, the station drawing power from a gas generator. They interspersed the delivery of messages and flood news with music from old seventy-eight rpm records found in storage at the transmitter.

Without electricity, the *Daily News-Miner* didn't publish for a week, but reporters and photographers kept working. More than a dozen people camped at the darkened newspaper plant, where reporter Lael Morgan created a cook stove from a five-gallon coffee can, using old newspapers for fuel. Realtor Ray Hill, one of about 3,500 people who sought shelter at the "Lathrop Hil-

Fairbanks Daily News-Miner

The flood caused catastrophic damage to many Fairbanks businesses.

ton," was remembered by all who saw him for his attire: blue bathrobe, red boots, and orange life vest.

About 4,000 people took shelter in homes on higher ground, with some single-family homes accommodating as many as twenty-five people. An armada of dozens of riverboats appeared from backyards and became the main means of transportation through the city. Frank and Neva Whaley pumped up two large aircraft tire tubes, tied them together and strapped a piece of plywood on top to make a boat with which they transported people to the airport.

Submerged fire hydrants, parking meters, fences, and other obstacles became navigation hazards in the cold muddy waters. Newspaperman Tom Snapp had to abandon his Volkswagen near the Polaris Building. With water halfway up the windshield, for some reason the wipers continued to run. One observer noted that some boat operators followed the traffic rules on the one-way streets. "Cruising through town was an experience I will never forget," college student Phil Deisher said. "We went by the Music Mart and there were guitars floating in the windows. The windows of Gordon's had been smashed out by the waves and chaos was a byword in all the stores."

Al George, civil defense director for the university, first expected that perhaps 700-800 people might seek refuge on the campus hill. But the campus population climbed to between 7,000 and 8,000, with refugees filling 27 buildings and creating a makeshift city in facilities designed to house 1,043 people. A nursery, an infirmary staffed by doctors and nurses who were among the flood victims, a kennel to care for 100 or so dogs, and even a daily newspaper called the *High Water News* appeared on campus. As the water receded the paper became the *(Lower) High Water News,* and the *(Even Lower) High Water News.* The refugees helped prepare 68,000 meals during the first week.

At the height of the flood, more than 1,500 volunteers responded to an emergency call to build a dike and keep the rising water from knocking out the University of Alaska power plant. Workmen siphoned gas from cars to run a pump to lower the water in the plant basement. A desperate thirteen-hour effort to save the power plant paid off when the water was stopped with only one-and-a-half inches to spare.

At the public safety building downtown, the main floor became a marina with boats coming in one door and going out another. Denali Elementary School became home to about two hundred people, who took to the second floor to stay dry. About a dozen people remained at St. Joseph's Hospital, using flashlights, candles, and two kerosene lamps to see at night. "When we had time to rest we listened to the water lapping at the floor we were standing on and the logs and debris bumping the joists as they floated by," said the hospital administrator. "This flood was a tremendous experience," she said. "I am not sorry to have been a part of it. Everyone shared. If your home was spared, you took in so many friends and neighbors that it was your home no longer. People were kind, extremely kind, and the needy proud had to accept. The water treated everything alike, modern house and old shack."

There were some reports of looting, but far more reports of people pulling together in the face of disaster and helping their neighbors. A local accountant became a KP worker; a banker did Salvation Army work. As the water receded and the river returned to normal, damage assessment began.

"This is undoubtedly a tragedy," said U.S. Senator E.L. "Bob" Bartlett. "But now the big job has to be done. We've got to get this city back in operation before the freezeup comes."

People spent weeks shoveling slimy silt from living rooms and sifting through trash to find personal possessions, surprised to find that not everything had been washed down to the Yukon River. Fairbanksans pumped out basements, replaced insulation, repainted, and repaired damaged homes and businesses. Every neighborhood looked like a big garage sale, with clothes, household goods, and furniture placed outside to dry.

Most businesses had no flood insurance and many lost much of their inventory. Dave Adler, the seventy-three-year-old owner of the bookstore known as the House of Adler, had to toss out 2,000 books and his office supplies. His bookstore had burned to the ground in 1948 and was damaged by fire another time, but he was resilient. "The fires didn't stop us and the flood won't bother us either," he said.

One of the few businesses with insurance was KTVF, Chan-

Fairbanks Daily News-Miner

The community effort initiating the hospital fund drive brought citizens together for the ground breaking. University of Alaska President William R. Wood headed the campaign.

nel 11, which was off the air for nearly four months. The insurance helped buy new equipment and KTVF returned to the air that winter to begin broadcasting in color for the first time. The entire town got a boost from the SBA, which didn't stand for "South Bound Alaskans," as one joke put it, but for the federal Small Business Administration, which provided tens of millions of dollars in loans at three percent interest. The 3,500 government loans to homeowners and businesses proved critical in disaster recovery.

By midwinter, a community consensus developed that something needed to be done about the flood-damaged St. Joseph's Hospital. The Sisters of Charity had announced more than a year earlier that the hospital would not be rebuilt. The religious order made it official in October 1967, after Fairbanks voters rejected, for the second time, a bond issue to build a new community hospital.

Out of this defeat, however, an impressive show of community spirit emerged. Various political factions put aside differences and combined forces to solve what had become an emergency. An executive committee led by Dr. William R. Wood, president of the University of Alaska, began raising funds privately to build a new hospital. Fairbanksans responded in generous fashion, doubling the original $1 million goal in less than three months. The successful drive created the momentum that ended with the completion of Fairbanks Memorial Hospital on Cowles Street, built with $2.6 million raised locally and $6 million in matching state and federal funds.

The flood also spurred action on developing a flood control project for Fairbanks. On an August morning six years after the flood, drizzling rain fell as Lt. Governor H.A. "Red" Boucher tossed a shovelful of dirt onto a front-end loader to begin the federally funded $275-million Chena River Lakes Flood Control Project, which reduced the flood threat. After completion, four thirty-ton steel gates on a dam upstream could be closed at times of high water to prevent downstream flooding. Since 1981, hydrologists estimate, the project has prevented more than $230 million in flood damage in Fairbanks.

Another lasting legacy of the flood is the inspiration derived from the community memory of a time when Fairbanksans met a crisis with courage and conviction. In 1969, Fairbanks received recognition as an All-America City, one of eleven cities to win the honor that year. The flood recovery and the hospital campaign stood out as examples of commitment to community, *Look* magazine and the National League of Cities said. "Only an all-out effort, with neighbor helping neighbor shovel, repair, and share, dug Fairbanks out in time," the judges said. "Emergency funds came from federal and state government and other U.S. cities, but all of Fairbanks—from bank presidents to day laborers to teachers to children—turned out to supply the muscle."

Fairbanksans looked back with pride on the events that began with high water in August 1967. "I was born in this town so you know how I feel," banker Bill Stroecker said upon hearing news of the All-America City award. "The people put out a tremendous effort under the most adverse conditions. The award is something the entire town deserves. In the gold mining days there was always the feeling that everyone was in the same boat. During the flood this was literally true." ■

Eva McGown, the Official Hostess of Fairbanks, helped countless thousands of people who needed a place to stay or someone to talk to.

Eva McGown, an Irish Lady with a Big Heart

She was the "living leprechaun" of Fairbanks, who put the heart in the Golden Heart City during her decades as the town's Official Hostess.

Her office was a corner desk in the Nordale Hotel lobby on Second Avenue, and she served a key role in the 1940s and early 1950s in finding places for people to stay in a town where there were no hotel rooms to be found. She could persuade people to take strangers into their homes and possessed enough charm "to coax the birds out of the trees," a friend said.

"I know of no more needed public service that is being rendered," newspaperman John Pegues wrote in 1946, after spending a day watching Eva help anyone who approached. "Nor do I know of anyone who could do it more graciously than Eva does."

Comments like "God Bless Ye," and "Now son, I'll be hearin' your problems," and "Shure and we'll be a-fixing ye up somehow" would emanate from her corner of the lobby even when the search for a bed seemed hopeless. She was a friend to homesick servicemen and worried wives and the best ambassador Fairbanks ever had, serving as hostess for more than three decades. A character in the novel *Ice Palace* was based on her and she once appeared on the *This Is Your Life* TV show.

Eva Montgomery came to Fairbanks from Ireland in 1914 and married Arthur McGown, part owner of the Model Cafe, the night she got off the stage from Chitina. Clara Rust, a longtime friend of Eva's, once said, "Thus, she was often called the 'mail order bride,' which she did not like at all."

Arthur took sick five years after the marriage and was an invalid for a decade before he died in 1930. "Then I learned about loneliness," Eva once said. "It is a heavier load than any woman can carry."

Eva never married again, but her life was rich and full. She began her unusual career simply by visiting lonely women who had just come to Alaska and tried to make them feel welcome, in a place where they were strangers. She visited patients at the hospital, met the trains departing for the South, and soon became involved in every aspect of life in Fairbanks.

Her friendly and outgoing manner evolved into a one-woman housing and greeting service that became vital during the many years when the demand for housing outstripped the supply.

Between 1940 and 1951 she helped about 50,000 new arrivals, construction workers, visitors, and students find shelter, according to a story about her life published in *Reader's Digest*. During World War II she received $75 a month from the Chamber of Commerce to run her housing office. Later she became an official city employee, drawing a $110 monthly salary.

Eva died in the fire that destroyed the Nordale Hotel, which had been her home for twenty-eight years. Writer Jo Anne Wold pointed out that one of the items found in the hotel safe after the fire was a box containing a piece of dried sod from Ireland, a reminder of the old country. ■

Grim-faced and weary Alaska Governor Wally Hickel, left, and Fairbanks Mayor H.A. "Red" Boucher waded through flood waters as they discuss coping with the disaster they faced.

16

The Oil Years in Alaska

Trucks lined up in Fairbanks to carry pieces of forty-eight-inch pipe for the construction of the Trans-Alaska Pipeline. The pipeline construction boom brought unprecedented changes.

George Preston, a Northern Commercial Co. manager, gave the commencement address to the Class of 1945 at Fairbanks High School. He said he worried that the graduates might be leaving school with the wrong notion about the work world because of what they had seen during the World War II boom in Fairbanks. The high-paying jobs they had enjoyed couldn't be expected to last. "Some of you—particularly some of the boys—during your vacations for the

199

past year or two, have been employed at jobs where you earned pay on the scale of bank presidents," he said. "You did not understand the full import of these things I am sure, and you possibly took it for granted that this was how it would always be."

Exactly thirty years later, a different generation of Fairbanks students, who attended Lathrop High School in five-hour shifts, heard a strikingly similar message from another commencement speaker. Another boom, another warning that this was not how it would always be. Students at the time attended high school either from 7 a.m. to noon or from 1 p.m. to 6 p.m., which left enough time to earn a sizable paycheck during the trans-Alaska pipeline boom.

"The double shift and the local job market have allowed many of you to hold full-time jobs while finishing school and frequently school has suffered from the competing demands on your time," English teacher Susan Stitham told the 1975 East Lathrop graduates. "Personally I think this is not good.

"What we are seeing in Fairbanks and Alaska is a clash of values, conflicting ideas on what is important for Alaska and our city," she said.

The clash of values and conflicting ideas about everything from money to crime in the streets highlighted another tumultuous era in Fairbanks history; when the city became a work camp for the largest private construction project in history. The pipeline emerged as the dominant fact of life because in 1968 on Alaska's North Slope, Atlantic Richfield discovered the largest oil field ever found in North America. Geologist Gill Mull wrote that the massive oil deposit "resulted from a one-in-a-million chance of a fortuitous combination of geological attributes that took at least 360 million years to form." Finding the oil was not a one-in-a-million proposition but it was a long shot, for there had been a series of costly North Slope exploration failures. After tapping into the giant Prudhoe Bay field in 1967-68 with what would have probably been the last exploratory well had it been a dry hole, the industry set about to quickly extract that which had taken hundreds of millions of years to form.

Combining forces in an assemblage known first as the Trans Alaska Pipeline System or TAPS, and later as Alyeska, the major oil companies ordered forty-eight-inch pipe from Japan and prepared to build a $900 million pipeline across Alaska. This came as welcome news to many people in Fairbanks, a town that was still drying out from the 1967 flood. Oil suddenly appeared as the economic hope of the future. "Fairbanks greeted the discovery of oil at Prudhoe Bay with cheers and a scramble to be ready for the dollars that were bound to flow in," one observer wrote.

The *Daily News-Miner*, an eager cheerleader for the oil industry, exemplified this attitude by saying that Fairbanks and Prudhoe Bay should go together like sugar and spice or Minneapolis and St. Paul. The newspaper said the town needed to go out of its way to persuade the companies to use the Golden Heart City as a supply and service center.

Pipeline boosters in Fairbanks didn't expect the project would be tied up in the courts and the federal bureaucracy for five years with disputes about Native land claims and the environment. Stopping the pipeline became the first great cause of a newly energized environmental movement in America. And the unresolved Native land claims issue emerged as a critical political and civil rights question that had to be settled before the pipeline progressed.

After a brief "false boom" following the oil discovery, the Fairbanks economy stagnated as the pipeline permit delay stretched from months to years. Many businesses had expanded their operations in expectation of immediate construction and they soon faced bills and payrolls they could not meet. The pipeline delay meant financial ruin for some who had gambled on the schedule and lost.

In light of the uncertain future of the project, the community never did much to prepare for a construction boom that might never happen. Victor Fischer, a researcher and former city planner in Anchorage, said at a 1976 conference this was in keeping with local tradition. He said Fairbanks didn't take steps to prepare for the pipeline because "Fairbanks has been and is anti-government, anti-planning, and the least organized community, probably, in the United States."

Borough government, which had been forced upon the populace by the Legislature in the 1960s, over the objections of local voters, exercised limited planning and zoning control over the vast area beyond the city limits during pipeline construction. "I hate to think what would have happened if the pipeline had come along before we had the expanded area under some control," said Borough Assembly member Bill Stringer. The lack of advance information from the oil companies about what would happen to Fairbanks also made the community gun-shy about investing large sums in improving facilities for a temporary boom.

A 1975 forum on local concerns led a visiting planner to comment that Fairbanksans didn't seem to have a shared vision about the community's future. "It's as if we all get aboard a 747 and are airborne and then the pilot comes out and asks us where we want to go, and everybody has a different idea," he said.

That may have had something to do with the reality that, as with the previous military buildup, the pipeline decisions were entirely out of the hands of people in Alaska. The pipeline didn't move past the talking stage until Congress settled Native land claims and took a major step into the fray over environmental issues. In 1973, Vice President Spiro Agnew, voting as Senate president, broke a 49-49 tie to approve an amendment that limited future court challenges to the project. On Jan. 23, 1974 the *News-Miner* printed a two-inch-high headline: "Pipeline Permit Signed! Line Permit—Key to Alaska's Future."

As 1974 rolled along, the rah-rah attitude that the Key to Alaska's Future would cure all ills began to crumble. The realization grew that in addition to money, the pipeline would bring things Fairbanks didn't want—crime, long lines at every store, more traffic, and other inconveniences. Michael Carey, a researcher studying Fairbanks' response to the boom, said that even at the Chamber of Commerce, he found mixed feelings. "They say they are concerned about how to keep the old Alaska, or what they regard as traditional Alaska, and at the same time have progress," he said in 1974.

By the end of construction, the pipeline's cost had climbed to $8 billion and the work force had peaked at 28,072. It took three years and two months to complete the pipeline, a period during which "pipeline impact" became a catch phrase to describe anything that happened.

Thousands of job seekers came to Fairbanks. The phone system ran out of numbers and the waiting list for new phones topped 1,500. The electric utilities managers warned that it would be best to buy a generator for backup power because their systems were stretched to capacity. Waiting in line and traffic jams became a way of life, despite the tantalizing wide-open spaces a mile or two from town. Alyeska, which spent about $800,000 a day in Fairbanks, occupied the North Post of Fort Wainwright, part of which had been vacated by Uncle Sam's army to become a temporary home to portions of "Uncle Al's" pipeline army. The soldiers in this army often wore pointy-toed boots and cowboy hats and arrived in town on the Alaska Airlines *Pipeline Express*, straight from Houston and Dallas.

Many people quit jobs in town to take better-paying pipeline jobs, leaving hard-to-fill vacancies in Fairbanks. The city police department lost most of its experienced officers, who went to work for the Alyeska security department. "What can we do?" said Fairbanks Police Capt. Lew Gibson. "We pay $1,600 a month; they're paying $1,600 a week." A banker joked about giving diamond seniority pins to clerks who stayed at least thirty days. The Fairbanks schools expected 3,000 additional students, but the pipeliners did not bring children with them and the schools, which had prepared for a full dose of "pipeline impact," saw a negligible enrollment increase.

The pipeline contractors became good customers for local businesses, sometimes too good. "Apparently no one else is going to try and put the brake on our purchasing policy as regards buying out an item in the Fairbanks area," Larry Carpenter, a Fairbanks newsman turned Alyeska spokesman wrote in a memo in August 1974. "Right now Fairbanks stores have no stock of water softener salt. A manager at a local supermarket told me 'Alyeska bought out everyone for the camps.' In recent weeks this has also been the story on batteries, ladders, four-wheel-drive vehicles, etc."

In the midst of this rush to build the pipeline, driven by the desire of the oil companies to start earning money on their multi-billion-dollar investment as soon as possible, Fairbanks businesses and many residents found that, at least financially, times had never been better. Food stamp use dropped by ninety percent. The number of businesses nearly doubled between 1973 and 1976. In those same years, the borough population climbed by more than forty percent, according to one study. Personal income for Fairbanks households nearly doubled in four years; pipeline work schedules that called for working forty hours or more of overtime every week inflated paychecks to new heights.

Dispatched through Fairbanks union halls to jobs up and down the line, blue collar workers earned wages that surpassed those of many college-educated professionals. Tales of big spending and high living became common currency, but many people didn't like the furor that overtook Fairbanks. In one major survey of public opinion, nearly half of those polled said they had personally gained during the pipeline, but only fourteen percent said the project changed Fairbanks for the better. "The pipeline has been a relentless, all-consuming activity, which has left people worn out and troubled and isolated from one another," one prominent minister said.

With new residents arriving in Fairbanks by the thousands, housing became impossible to find. Among the rental listings advertised in 1975 were: two rooms and two five-gallon water jugs for $500 a month; an unfinished house with no water for $700 a month; a hallway that had been turned into a $300-a-month apartment; and truck campers in parking lots. The manager of McDonald's allowed some of his employees to sleep in his Winnebago; others camped for the summer in a park near the restaurant and used his home for showers. Even so, employee turnover in the summer of 1975 was 200 percent, as teenagers could easily find other jobs.

Traffic congestion worsened and prostitutes openly walked the downtown streets in a daily spectacle that drew news coverage around the world. Not long after World War II a *Chicago Tribune* reporter who visited Fairbanks wrote, "Second Avenue in Fairbanks is probably as wild and wide open as any little street in the postwar world." *Jessen's Weekly* responded that the reporter hadn't been in Fairbanks "in the wartime years, so he can't be expected to appreciate the difference between those hectic days and these times of comparative peace and quiet."

During pipeline construction, Second Avenue set a new standard for "hectic days," with standing-room-only crowds in the bars that lined the little street. On the few blocks the pipeliners called "Two Street," work-

Fairbanks Daily-News-Miner

Airport Way, one of several four-lane highways in the city, aided the development of commercial and residential centers away from the downtown core area.

ers with $1,000 or more to spend on R&R could find anything except comparative peace and quiet.

The impact of all this commotion created a deep gulf among Alaskans about the pace of progress. Governor Jay Hammond, elected in 1974 on what his critics claimed was a "no-growth" platform, said in a Fairbanks speech, "Half of Alaska seems to view each oil province as the Holy Grail, while the other half perceives it as a cup of bitter vetch." He said the challenge for Alaska was to "hold trauma to the tolerable and retain at least some semblance of a sane lifestyle." One Fairbanksan who had found a sane lifestyle impossible to hold onto summed up his view of the pipeline to the borough's Impact Information Center by saying, "Prices too high. Traffic bad. Pollution terrible.

"Being an old timer from territorial days, I resent the influx of rabble looking for the easy buck and caring little for our traditions," he said.

Another view, this one from the *Anchorage Times*, said the "discombobulation" brought by pipeline construction was all a matter of temporary inconvenience. "Alaskans are in a period of improvement that can be compared to a residential subdivision which is having a sewer system installed," the newspaper said. The long-run benefits would accrue to the state after the pipeline was completed, just as a subdivision benefits when the ditches are filled and the inconvenience of construction is "merely a footnote of the past."

The ground zero of footnotes was downtown Fairbanks, a neighborhood already in need of rehabilitation before the project began. There had been numerous plans to "save" downtown, the most ambitious being an $80 million enclosed mall stretching from First to Seventh Avenue and Cushman to Barnette Streets. Though endorsed by the city council in 1974, the proposed mall never saw a shopper. A 1972 study had called for aggressive action to keep downtown, where the largest department stores were J.C. Penney and the NC Co., as the retail center of the community through transportation and land planning. The study proposed five parking garages and several enclosed pedestrian walkways, which would be heated to forty degrees in winter to keep shoppers comfortable.

The grand schemes never materialized and downtown continued to deteriorate to the point where many people said Fairbanks had no downtown left at all by the late 1970s. "What is happening here is the developer is making the decision for the community, that the community is not going to have a downtown." Sue Fison, director of the borough Impact Information Office, said in 1976. Developers decided that the traffic, parking, and the neighborhood conditions made a move to the malls good business. The customers eagerly followed, no longer having to fight the traffic on the narrow streets.

Many retail businesses migrated to the malls built away from downtown, a trend that began with the opening of Foodland and the Gavora Mall and continued with the Bentley Mall, Shoppers Forum, University Center, and Fred Meyer. The growth of the new commercial centers and the building of new highways and other public facilities, many of them completed after the boom had ended, made it much easier to live and work in Fairbanks, particularly in the suburbs.

Still, a town does not survive on strip malls and shopping centers alone. For two decades and more, the question of how best to redevelop the center of downtown Fairbanks remained a central issue in city politics. Solutions proved elusive. Repeated attempts to attract a major hotel and convention center downtown failed. With millions in state grants, the city installed modern underground utilities, demolished most of the bars downtown and replaced them with "temporary" parking lots. Several new downtown enterprises proved viable and a park opened, but the parking lots on sites once frequented by bar-hopping pipeliners proved to have a longer life span than anyone had expected. Fairbanks neared its centennial while making progress on several new initiatives to create a more vibrant city center.

The pace of business downtown had dropped off in 1977 not only because of the new malls that emerged as the main centers for retail shopping, but also because once the oil started flowing in the pipe at five to six miles an hour, the construction workers went home, and Fairbanks took a breather. The slowdown lasted for a couple of years.

But then another Mideast oil crisis raised the price of Alaska oil and the state began earning additional billions of dollars in taxes and royalties. Alaskans again found themselves in the strange position of benefiting from actions by OPEC that did overall damage to the U.S. economy. When oil prices hit their peak, the state was spending more than $10,000 annually for every Alaska resident, paying for services funded in many other states by local tax dollars or private groups.

Scrutiny of state spending disappeared during the legislative spending spree of the early 1980s and the public raised few objections. Through a lengthy catalog of low-interest loans, grants, tax credits, and other measures to redistribute the wealth, the state poured millions of dollars into the economy. Alaska eliminated its state income tax and began giving annual checks to every resident, the cumulative payments from which totaled more than $15,000 for those who collected every check from 1982-1998.

Local government, particularly the borough, gained a rich new tax base from the oil pipeline and the North Pole Refinery, and the community grew. The 1998 borough population was estimated at 84,000, an increase of 25,000 or more from 1980. Most of the growth took place outside the city limits in the growing suburbs of Fairbanks that stretched farther and farther into the surrounding countryside.

The oil money spent by the state in the years since the pipeline began operation created more "pipeline impact" than pipeline construction did, but it didn't happen all at once.

Following the ascent, came the descent. In 1986, when Saudi Arabia increased production and oil prices dipped, the Fairbanks economy tumbled. Several major Alaska banks failed, construction almost stopped, and bankruptcies and foreclosures multiplied as thousands of people couldn't pay their bills. The overheated real estate market cooled off as fast as a stalled car at fifty below. Many people suddenly found that they owed more on their mortgages than their houses were worth and those who sold out often had to write sizable checks at the time of sale to cover the difference.

An expansion at Fort Wainwright somewhat alleviated the recession, but Fairbanks lost about 3,000 jobs in three years. Money spent on the Exxon Valdez cleanup and higher oil prices helped revive the economy in the early 1990s, but by decade's end oil prices had dropped once more, and oil production was in sharp decline leading some people to marvel at the staying power of the boom and bust cycle that had started with E.T. Barnette and Felix Pedro. ■

Epilogue

More than 3,000 runners and walkers line up for the annual Midnight Sun Run held during the longest weekend of the year in late June when it never gets dark.

A visiting Washington correspondent arrived in Fairbanks in 1906 to find a town with several muddy streets, some painted buildings, attractive log cabins, telephone service that compared favorably with East Coast cities, and something else. "The people of Fairbanks are confident of the future," Walter Clark wrote,

209

"for they believe that the mining region tributary to their city will still be productive a century from now." Of all the predictions made about Fairbanks over the past century—that it would one day be the St. Louis or the Chicago or the Ohio of the North, this one by the newsman and future Alaska governor may come closest to hitting the truth. Clark visited Fairbanks a few months after fire nearly destroyed it, a calamity the town withstood because it was at the center of the richest gold mining region in Alaska. Nearly a century has passed and Fairbanks, though repeatedly rising and falling with economic, political, and natural forces beyond its control, remains a place where people seek their fortunes, financial and otherwise.

The gold rush of the early days brought a bonanza that temporarily created one of the richest towns on earth. Gold production never again reached the heights of those early years, but in the 1990s, the industry came back to life in Fairbanks. At the half-billion-dollar Fort Knox gold mine, twenty-five road miles northeast of Fairbanks, machinery rumbles twenty-four hours a day. The mine, which produces about a ton of gold a month, combines the microscopic with the mammoth because there is one ounce of gold in every forty tons of rock. To haul the ore, the mine uses 150-ton trucks the size of two-story houses.

The mine has giant screened revolving cylinders in which steel balls the size of shot puts or larger tumble onto the gold-bearing rock in a deafening roar. The steel balls break up the rock into fine particles so the gold can be recovered, but the balls wear out fast. Every day the mine adds thirty tons of new steel balls to the rock-crushing cylinders.

Yet, the Fort Knox mine represents only a small part of Fairbanks' economy today. The University of Alaska Fairbanks, Fairbanks International Airport, the Army, the Air Force, Doyon Ltd., the Tanana Chiefs Conference, Alyeska Pipeline Service Co., and the Alaska Railroad are among the other major economic influences in the community. About four out of every ten people in the work force, including a sizable military contingent, are employed by the various levels of government. Public spending is a key to the economy, as is the business of supplying everything from automobiles to xylophones to the 80,000 area residents.

It is a town of contradictions where politics sometimes resembles hand-to-hand combat. Taxes are low, complaints about government are high, and the schools consistently draw high marks from parents. During the upheaval and

Jimmy Bedford

Pope John Paul II and President Ronald Reagan met in Fairbanks on a cool day in May 1984. The pontiff signed a shirt for one resident "JPII."

sudden growth brought by the construction of the trans-Alaska pipeline, downtown Fairbanks deteriorated into a skid row before beginning a long and slow recovery. There have been attempts to preserve parts of Fairbanks' past, most notably in the creation of Alaskaland, where old cabins populate Gold Rush Town and the stern-wheeler *Nenana* spends its retirement years. But throughout the years, Fairbanks has been impatient to tear down the old and build anew, without much thought for city planning or what somebody else might think.

A late 1940s tourist brochure expressed the image that Fairbanks liked to project: "As you walk the streets of Fairbanks, you can envision days past when the city was a rough-and-tumble gold mining camp, living by and for the precious metal. But this vision is interrupted time and again by modern homes, new businesses; and there comes the realization that here is a young metropolis, the economic axis on which turns the future of Interior Alaska. Great gold mining companies, multi-crop farms, a productive fur industry, lumbering, the University of Alaska, a modern and complete business-shopping district, a vast hunting domain which beckons the stalker of bear and moose, awe-inspiring hills and streams—THIS is Fairbanks today."

As you walk the streets of Fairbanks today, it takes a great deal more imagination to envision the rough-and-tumble gold mining camp of the past, except in a couple of neighborhoods where old cabins are still the main architectural influence. The rest is a western hodgepodge that reflects an innate desire to build whatever one wants wherever one wants, a streak that is as much a community standard as talking about the weather during the extreme lows of winter and the highs of summer. In a town where there have been many transients, tradition and a sense of history can be as elusive as a wolf in the wild. There is an eagerness by some to get away from restrictions or thinking that may have bound them in the Lower 48, while there is also a tendency to recreate Fairbanks in the image of every place else.

The town's unique character, bred in isolation, has been gradually evolving into something more familiar, under the pressure of cable television, shopping malls, instant phone access, more movies, more radio stations, the Internet, easy airline access, and other factors that tend to make distances irrelevant and end seclusion.

Today, when an old-timer goes Outside, he won't get a sendoff anything like that accorded Louis Golden early in the century. When Golden went Outside for the first time in nineteen years, his friends threw a party and gave him a bell and a strap to hang around his neck that had the words, "This is Louis Golden of Fairbanks Alaska. Return C.O.D. after 90 Days." A small-town atmosphere survives against the encroachment brought by the anonymity of urban and suburban sprawl, but there are others who look back fondly to the time when everyone knew everyone. The late Maury Smith, a popular Fairbanks journalist who served as the "Hometown Reporter" for a quarter-century on radio, TV, and in the pages of local newspapers, believed the main change occurred starting in World War II. Many of the people who moved to Fairbanks after that time "brought the states with them, trying to make Alaska like the Lower 48," he said in 1973. "All this sounds as if I might be against progress, but one must define what he means by progress," Smith said. "It isn't all concrete and steel. It really is a way of living."

Fort Wainwright soldiers, wearing winter gear, line up to board a C-130 for an arctic training mission in 1988, dubbed "Callous Warrior I."

Despite all the changes and turmoil, thousands still find the way of living better than any other place on earth. There are any number of service organizations that rely on the donation of countless hours of volunteer time. People are willing to help others. You notice this mainly during bouts with severe winter weather, when the cold can be life-threatening. In my own case, I'll never forget the helpfulness of a couple of dozen neighbors and the firefighters of the Steese Volunteer Fire Department who kept my house from burning down one spring day.

Fairbanks is a town where often is heard a discouraging word about gun control, where hunters are not an endangered species and weekend dog mushers may double as doctors, lawyers, laborers, or string players in the symphony orchestra. There are churches where faiths of many kinds are practiced, including what is known in some quarters as the "Church of the Blue Sky," heavily attended on sunny summer Sundays.

People without much building experience still teach themselves to build their own houses, often starting in cabins without indoor plumbing. There are painters, sculptors, and actors among those present who share their talents in local shops, festivals, and through community theater, which survives despite the onslaught of electronic media.

Top college baseball players swing for the fences at Growden Park in the Alaska League of summer baseball, while at fields that are not much farther than a long home run away you'll find ten-year-old Little Leaguers doing the same. A couple of thousand kids play soccer on summer evenings and a couple of thousand parents cheer them on. In the winter, curlers and hockey players take to the ice, while dog mushers, skiers, and snowmachiners don't have far to go to seek the snow. Others sit by the fire and wait for the midnight sun, dreaming of days without nights.

W.F. Thompson, the first editor of the *News-Miner*, analyzed the future prospects for Fairbanks during one of its down times by saying that attitude is all-important in every era and the "Gospel of Hope beats the Religion of Despair by a considerable margin." Nearly one hundred years has elapsed since the accidental grounding of E.T. Barnette and the gold discovery by Felix Pedro. The evidence of the first century in Fairbanks would seem to prove that Thompson was right. The Gospel of Hope survives.

Fairbanks Daily News-Miner

Artists Anita Tabor , left, and Stan Zielinski carve a dall sheep from a block of ice.

214

L. W. Nelson

Bibliography

Over the years I have benefited from the generous assistance of many people in Fairbanks who have helped me learn the history of Alaska's Golden Heart City. I would like to thank them all. In writing a daily newspaper column, I come into contact with people from all walks of life who have interesting insights on the development of Fairbanks.

This book touches on some of the highlights in Fairbanks' history mixed with anecdotes that I hope will reveal something about the character of the place and its people.

I want to thank the *Fairbanks Daily News-Miner*, particularly Kelly Bostian, Paul Massey, and Chuck Gray. I am grateful for the efforts of editor Stephen Lay, whose hours of careful attention proved to be of great help. My brother Terrence offered good advice, and I'm glad he finally had a chance to use one of his favorite lines in the foreword.

Alaskana collector Candy Waugaman helped immeasurably with photos. I am thankful for the skilled staff of the archives of the Rasmuson Library at the University of Alaska Fairbanks, especially Gretchen Lake. Among the people who have helped me along the way with stories about history or writing advice are: Bill Stroecker, Bruce Haldeman, Steve Arthur, Phyllis Movius, Michael Carey, Claus Naske, Sam Bishop, Renee Blahuta, John Hewitt, Paul Solka, Pat Cook, Olga Steger, Lael Morgan, Richard Wien, and Kent Sturgis.

The sources of this book include newspaper accounts, books, magazine articles, interviews and archival materials. The *Fairbanks Daily News-Miner* and its predecessors were the most useful, along with *Jessen's Weekly* and the *Pioneer All-Alaska Weekly.*

The following is a partial list of books and academic reports consulted:

Boswell, John. *History of Alaskan Operations of United States Smelting, Refining, and Mining Company*. Fairbanks: University of Alaska, Mineral Industries Research Laboratory, 1979.

Cashen, William. *Farthest North College President: Charles E. Bunnell and the Early History of the University of Alaska*. Fairbanks: University of Alaska Press, 1972.

Cloe, John with Michael Monaghan. *Top Cover for America*. Missoula, MT: Pictorial Histories Publishing Co., 1984.

Cole, Terrence. *Crooked Past: The History of a Frontier Mining Camp*, Fairbanks, Alaska. Fairbanks: University of Alaska Press, 1991
—— *The Cornerstone on College Hill: An Illustrated History of the University of Alaska Fairbanks*. Fairbanks: University of Alaska Press, 1994.

Cooley, Richard. Fairbanks, *Alaska: A Survey of Progress*. Juneau: Alaska Development Board, July 1954.

Davis, Neil. *The College Hill Chronicles: How the University of Alaska Came of Age*. Fairbanks: University of Alaska Foundation, 1992.

Dixon, Mim. *What Happened to Fairbanks? The Effects of the Trans-Alaska Oil Pipeline on the Community of Fairbanks, Alaska*. Boulder, Colo.: Westview Press, 1978.

Kitchener, L.D. *Flag Over the North; The Story of the Northern Commercial Company*. Seattle: Superior Publishing Company, 1954.

Kruse, John A. *Fairbanks Community Survey. Fairbanks:* Institute of Social and Economic Research, 1976.

Movius, Phyllis. *The Role of Women in the Founding and Development of Fairbanks, Alaska, 1903-1923*. M.A. Thesis. University of Alaska Fairbanks. 1996

Naske, Claus, and Rowinski, L. J. *Fairbanks: A Pictorial History*. Virginia Beach, Va.: The Donning Company, 1981.

Patty, Ernest. *North Country Challenge*. New York: David McKay, 1949.

Potter, Jean. *Alaska Under Arms*. New York: Macmillan, 1942.
—— *The Flying North*. New York: Macmillan, 1947.

Rickard, T.A. *Through the Yukon and Alaska*. San Francisco: Mining and Scientific Press, 1909.

Robe, Cecil. *The Penetration of an Alaskan Frontier, The Tanana Valley and Fairbanks*. Ph. D. dissertation, Yale University, 1943.

Wickersham, James. *Old Yukon*. Washington, D.C.: Washington Law Book Co., 1938.

Wold, Jo Anne. *This Old House*. Anchorage, Alaska: Alaska Northwest Publishing Co., 1976.
—— *Fairbanks: The $200 Million Gold Rush Town*. Fairbanks, Alaska: Wold Press, 1971.

Index

About the Author

Dermot Cole is a longtime columnist for the *Fairbanks Daily News-Miner*. He is fascinated by the history of Alaska and has written extensively on the subject for more than 20 years.

Cole grew up in Pennsylvania and lived in Taiwan and Montana before moving to Fairbanks in 1974.

He studied journalism at the University of Alaska Fairbanks and was named a Michigan Journalism Fellow in 1986 by the University of Michigan. He also worked for the Associated Press in Seattle.

Cole lives outside of Fairbanks with his wife, journalist Debbie Carter, and their three children, Connor, Aileen and Anne. They enjoy cross-country skiing in the winter, the northern lights and believe that Fairbanks is a good place to raise a family.

Cole is the author of three other books: *Frank Barr: Bush Pilot in Alaska and the Yukon; Hard Driving: The 1908 Auto Race from New York to Paris;* and *Amazing Pipeline Stories: How Building the trans-Alaska Pipeline Transformed Life in America's Last Frontier.*